WOOD DECKS
Materials, Construction, and Finishing

by

Kent A. McDonald, Research Wood Scientist
Robert H. Falk, Structural Engineer
R. Sam Williams, Supervisory Research Chemist
Jerrold E. Winandy, Research Wood Scientist
U.S. Department of Agriculture, Forest Service
Forest Products Laboratory
Madison, Wisconsin

Acknowledgements

Several individuals and organizations contributed to the development and publication of this manual. The American Forest and Paper Association's Wood Deck Design Task Group oversaw the development of the structural design tables. This group included Cathy Marx (Southern Forest Products Association), Brad Douglas (American Forest and Paper Association), Jeff Fantozzi (formerly of Western Wood Products Association), Linda Brown (Southern Pine Inspection Bureau), Don DeVisser (West Coast Lumber Inspection Bureau), Charles Jourdain (California Redwood Association), and Eric Jones (Canadian Wood Council). We would like to thank them for their time and effort.

Several individuals provided excellent comments and suggestions to the manual. They include Thomas Daniels (Samual Cabot Inc.), K.J. McClelland (Western Red Cedar Lumber Association), Don Luebs (National Association of Home Builders Research Center), Frank Annessi (Hickson Corp.), and Jeff Easterling and Marc Lishewski (Southern Forest Products Association).

Thanks also go to Mary Collet (USDA Forest Service, Forest Products Laboratory) for her excellent editing job, Clay Bridge (Flad & Associates) for developing the CAD figures, and Art Brauner and Susan Stamm (Forest Products Society) for publishing this manual.

Cover photo courtesy of California Redwood Association.

▲ ▲ ▲ ▲ ▲ ▲ ▲ ▲ ▲ ▲ ▲ ▲ ▲ ▲ ▲ ▲ ▲ ▲ ▲

TABLE OF CONTENTS

Introduction

Every year, the number of decks built in America increases. This popularity has resulted not only from the desire to enhance outdoor living, but also from the relative simplicity of these structures, which allows do-it-yourself construction.

Though decks are relatively simple from a construction standpoint, they are outdoor structures and are unprotected from the rigors of the weather. Therefore, special attention is required in selecting materials, in construction methods and procedures, and in finishing a deck to assure the best possible performance.

Several publications are available in the marketplace that describe deck architecture, layout, and construction sequences. The primary goal of this manual is to provide information on the lumber appropriate for deck construction, construction details and sizing for structural integrity, and guidelines for finishing and maintaining a wood deck for appearance and longevity. The intent is to provide enough information so that the deck builder can better understand why deck materials perform the way they do, how to avoid or minimize potential maintenance problems, and how to correct problems.

There are few absolute rules for the construction and maintenance of wood decks; rather, there are several options, where the best solution is influenced by many factors.

These include local weather and site conditions, aesthetics, personal taste, and material availability and cost. Background information on the known properties of wood and wood behavior is included so that the deck builder can understand the rationale for recommendations. Information from other sources was examined and an attempt is made to provide clear recommendations where conflicting or misleading information exists.

The first two chapters define basic terminology and provide some basic information on wood properties relevant to the lumber available for wood deck construction. These chapters also include information on lumber grades and preservative treatment standards. Chapter 3 describes the structural design of wood decks, focusing on post, beam, and joist sizing. This chapter also describes fastener selection and construction details best suited for exposed wood construction. Chapter 4 describes the finishing (staining or sealing) of wood decks and provides information on enhancing long-term performance. Chapter 5 outlines inspection and maintenance procedures for existing decks.

The information provided in this publication assumes the outdoor construction use of naturally decay-resistant softwood species such as redwood and western cedars, and preservative-treated species such as pine, hemlock, fir, and Douglas-fir.

1

▲ ▲ ▲ ▲ ▲ ▲ ▲ ▲ ▲ ▲ ▲ ▲ ▲ ▲ ▲ ▲ ▲ ▲ ▲ ▲

WOOD STRUCTURE, MATERIAL PROPERTIES, AND LUMBER SELECTION

The following discussion of the structure and properties of wood provides background for understanding how lumber is graded, and how to select the best lumber for a deck. This introduction serves as a basis for discussing long-term durability, structural design, and finishing.

Wood Structure

Many factors affect the properties of lumber, including the location and orientation of the board cut from the log, and the presence of naturally-occurring characteristics, such as knots, checks, splits, and bark. In the following discussion, special terms pertaining to wood are defined, such as earlywood, latewood, heartwood, sapwood, vertical-grained, and flat-grained. This information is useful for understanding how to use wood in decks and how to interpret its behavior.

Wood Cells

As trees grow, wood cells form just below the bark during the spring and summer growing seasons. These wood cells are hollow tubular structures, primarily consisting of cellulose and hemicellulose, which are held firmly in place by a natural adhesive called lignin. The wood cells are much longer than they are wide and are tapered at the ends. Water can move from one cell to another through small openings between cells in softwoods or through vessels in hardwoods. The thickness of the wood cell walls increases as new cells are formed during a single growing season. The change in cell wall thickness each year produces the characteristic concentric growth rings visible in most tree species.

Growth Rings

Growth rings are most easily seen on a cross-sectional view of a log (Fig. 1). The portion of the growth ring formed during the spring (earlywood or springwood) is usually less dense than the portion formed during the summer (latewood or summerwood). The most drastic density change occurs at the junction of the latewood of one growing season and the earlywood of the next (Fig. 1). The width of the growth

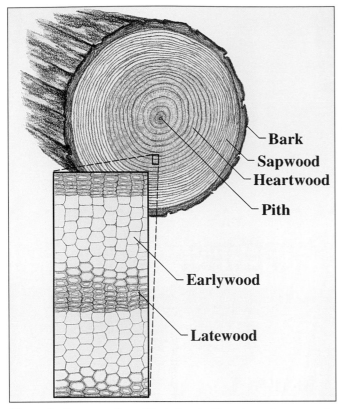

Figure 1. Cross-section of log showing heartwood, sapwood, earlywood, latewood, and pith.

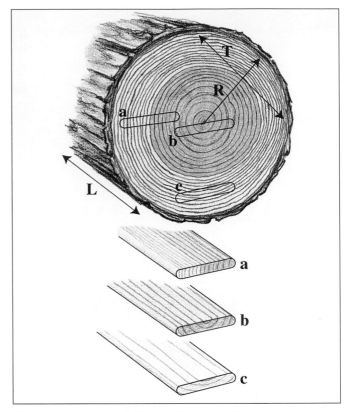

Figure 2. Grain orientations of log and of lumber cut from log.

layer, the thickness of individual cell walls, and the properties of these cells depend on the species, the weather during the growing season, the site where the tree is growing, and the age of the tree.

Cell Orientation

Most wood cells are oriented parallel to the longitudinal axis or main stem of a log. Because of this, wood has different properties in this direction than it does perpendicular to this axis of the log. The properties of wood are therefore referenced to three principle directions: 1) the longitudinal direction, which is along the length of the log, 2) the radial direction, which is from the center of the log out to the bark and perpendicular to the longitudinal direction, and 3) the tangential direction, which is perpendicular to the radial and longitudinal directions (see Fig. 2-L, R, T).

Lumber Orientation

The grain orientation of the lumber is established when the lumber is sawn from a log; the grain orientation depends on the location of the piece in the log (Fig. 2). The two extremes of grain orientation are flat-grained (Fig. 2, c) and edge-grained (sometimes called vertical-grained) (Fig. 2, a). The grain orientation of most lumber cut from the log is between these extremes. The board cut from the center of the log contains the pith (Fig. 2, b).

Heartwood and Sapwood

As a tree grows and new cells are added to the sapwood region, the older sapwood cells gradually change to heartwood. The transition from sapwood to heartwood is visible in the log cross-section as an apparent difference in color between the darker central heartwood portion of the log compared with the lighter outer sapwood portion (Fig. 1). Although both heartwood and sapwood provide the structural support for the tree, they serve different functions with regard to its life processes. Water and nutrient transport takes place within the inner bark and sapwood portion of the tree and is the life support system of the tree. The heartwood is not involved in moisture transport. It serves only as structural support and a storage area for many organic chemicals produced by the living tree.

The species-specific chemicals stored in the heartwood are called extractives. These chemicals give each wood species its characteristic properties, such as color and natural decay resistance. Although a few species, such as redwood and the western cedars, have a reputation for natural decay-resistance, the heartwood of these species provides the most durability because of its high concentration of certain extractives. Heartwood consists of dead wood cells, and the openings (which initially provided for lateral fluid transport between sapwood cells) often no longer function. Thus, the heartwood is very resistant to water movement. Except for a small amount of end-grain penetration, the heartwood surfaces (tangential and radial) are rather resistant to water movement compared with sapwood surfaces.

Juvenile Wood

The wood formed during the first few years of a tree's growth (8 to 10 years for some species) is called juvenile wood. This wood surrounds the pith, or center, of the tree. The pith can most easily be seen on the end grain of a log (Fig. 1) and sometimes on lumber (Fig. 2, b). In some species, this pith-related juvenile wood has abnormal properties and may cause large dimensional changes (generally in the longitudinal direction). These dimensional changes can cause severe warping of lumber. While mature wood does not significantly change (<0.1 percent) in longitudinal dimension between the green and dry states, juvenile wood can change up to 2.5 percent, which can result in wood shrinking more than 3

inches in a 12-foot board (Fig. 3). With dimensional change of this magnitude, juvenile wood may split, bow, twist, cup, and/or crook, and fasteners may be pulled out.

Knots

Knots result from branches and/or limbs growing on the main stem (bole) of the tree. As the tree gets older, the limbs remain alive, die, decay, or fall off the tree. Before the limb falls off, part of it may be encased by subsequent growth of the tree. In large trees, most of these encased branches are located in the central portion of the tree so that the lumber cut from the outer part of these trees is usually relatively free of knots. In smaller trees, these branches extend into the sapwood and most lumber from these trees will contain knots.

Knots resulting from living branches (tight knots) are typically intergrown and will remain an integral part of the surrounding wood. Those that result from dead branches are surrounded by, but not connected to the growing wood, which can result in loose knots or knot holes.

Knots radiate from the pith at the center of softwood trees and can vary in size and shape depending on the orientation of the sawcut when the lumber was produced. Knot form, size, quality (intergrown or loose), and frequency are considered when the lumber is graded and sorted for marketing.

Moisture Effects

In general, wood shrinks as it loses moisture and swells as it gains moisture. More precisely, wood only changes dimension between an absolutely dry state (completely free of moisture) and its fiber saturation point (the point at which the wood fibers are completely saturated with moisture). This fiber saturation point typically occurs at about 30 percent moisture content for most species. At this point, all the water in the wood is bound within the cell wall. As moisture content changes above the fiber saturation point, the cell cavities take on or lose unbound water, but the wood cell walls do not change in dimension. Below the fiber

Figure 3. Warping (top) and excessive surface degradation (bottom) resulting from juvenile wood.

saturation point, however, the wood does change dimension with changing moisture content. The amount of this change is dependent on the species and is always different for the three axes: radial, tangential, and longitudinal.

Table 1 gives the average dimensional change for several wood species along two axes. The longitudinal dimensional change of wood is essentially zero compared with that of the radial and tangential directions. This table shows that wood is more stable

in the radial direction than in the tangential direction. This is the reason why edge-grained (or vertical-grained) lumber is more desirable than lumber with other grain orientations. Figure 2 shows the grain orientation of edge-grained and flat-grained lumber.

Cup—One form of warp, cup, is the distortion of a board flatwise from a straight line across the width of the board. Cup occurs when shrinkage is unequal between two faces of a board, such as the top and bottom of a decking board. The tendency of a board to cup varies with its density, moisture content when surfaced, width, thickness, and grain orientation. Cup is more pronounced in flat-grained boards than in edge-grained boards.

Raised grain and shelling—Raised grain is a roughened condition of the surface of dressed lumber in which the harder latewood is raised above the softer earlywood but not torn loose from it; raised grain is comparable to a corrugated surface. In deck lumber, raised grain is usually caused by the cyclic wetting and drying of the surface, resulting in differential swelling and shrinking of the latewood and earlywood bands of individual annual rings.

Shelling, the separation or peeling of wood along the annual rings, is often the result of the same changing moisture content conditions that cause raised grain. However, shelling is the failure of and separation of the wood between the latewood and earlywood bands. Shelling is more prone to occur on the pith side rather than the bark side of flatsawn lumber (Fig. 4).

Commercial Lumber for Decks

In a broad sense, commercial lumber is any lumber that is bought or sold in the normal channels of commerce. Many wood species are grouped for marketing purposes. The species often used for deck construction are listed in Table 2. Lumber may be found in a variety of forms, species, and types, and in various commercial establishments, both wholesale and retail. Most commercial lumber is graded by standard

Table 1. Shrinkage values of domestic woods.

Wood species	Shrinkage from green to ovendry moisture content[a]	
	Radial	Tangential
Western cedars		
Alaska	2.8	6.0
Incense	3.3	5.2
Port Orford	4.6	6.9
Western redcedar	2.4	5.0
Douglas–fir[b]		
Coast	4.8	7.6
Interior North	3.8	6.9
Interior West	4.8	7.5
Southern pine		
Loblolly	4.8	7.4
Longleaf	5.1	7.5
Shortleaf	4.6	7.7
Slash	5.4	7.6
Ponderosa pine	3.9	6.2
Redwood		
Old–growth	2.6	4.4
Young–growth	2.2	4.9

[a] Shrinkage is expressed as a percentage of green dimension.

[b] Coast Douglas-fir is defined as Douglas-fir growing in Oregon and Washington west of the Cascade Mountains summit. Interior West includes California and all counties in Oregon and Washington east of, but adjacent to, the Cascade summit. Interior North includes the remainder of Oregon and Washington and Idaho, Montana, and Wyoming.

Figure 4. Example of shelling: separation between earlywood and latewood bands.

Table 2. Species groups for deck construction.

Species group	Species included in group	Grading rules-writing agencies
Douglas Fir–Larch	Douglas-fir Western larch	WCLIB WWPA
Hem–Fir	California red fir Grand fir Noble fir Pacific silver fir Western hemlock White fir	WCLIB WWPA
Ponderosa pine	Ponderosa pine	NLGA WCLIB WWPA
Redwood	Redwood	RIS
Southern Pine	Loblolly pine Longleaf pine Shortleaf pine Slash pine	SPIB
Spruce–Pine–Fir	Alpine fir Balsam fir Black spruce Engelmann spruce Jack pine Lodgepole pine Red spruce White spruce	NLGA
Spruce–Pine–Fir (South)	Balsam fir Black spruce Jack pine Norway (red) pine Red spruce White spruce	NELMA NSLB
	Engelmann spruce Lodgepole pine Sitka spruce	WCLIB WWPA
Western cedars	Alaska cedar Incense cedar Port–Orford cedar Western redcedar	NLGA WCLIB WWPA

NELMA—Northeastern Lumber Manufacturers Association, NLGA—National Lumber Grades Authority, NSLB—Northern Softwood Lumber Bureau, RIS—Redwood Inspection Service, SPIB—Southern Pine Inspection Bureau, WCLIB—West Coast Lumber Inspection Bureau, WWPA—Western Wood Products Association

rules that make purchasing quite uniform throughout the country.

A sawn log yields lumber of varying quality. To enable users to buy the quality that best suits their purposes, lumber is graded into use categories, each with an appropriate range of quality.

Generally, the grade of a piece of lumber is based on the number, character, and location of growth characteristics that may affect the strength or the utility value of the lumber. Among the more common visual characteristics are knots, checks, pitch pockets, shake, and stain. Some of these characteristics are found in the growing tree. Some lumber grades are free or practically free of these characteristics. Other grades, which constitute the great bulk of lumber, contain knots and other characteristics. Lumber containing such characteristics is entirely satisfactory for many uses, as long as it is properly graded.

Grading of most lumber takes place at the sawmill. Establishment of grading procedures is largely the responsibility of lumber grading agencies. Because of the wide variety of wood species, industrial practices, and customer needs, different lumber grading practices coexist. The grading practices that are pertinent to deck designers and builders are considered in the sections that follow.

Structural Grades

Most softwood lumber nominally 2 to 4 inches thick (called dimension lumber) and some lumber greater than 5 inches thick (called timber) is stress graded and called structural lumber. Stress-graded lumber is assigned allowable properties under the National Grading Rule (NGR), a part of the American Softwood Lumber Standard.[1] For stress-graded dimension lumber, a single set of grade names and descriptions is used throughout the United States, although the assigned allowable properties may vary with species or species group (Fig. 5, Table 3).

Visual stress grading is based on the premise that the strength of any piece of structural lumber depends on the strength-

---

[1] *U.S. Department of Commerce. 1994. American Softwood Lumber Standard PS 20-94. Washington, DC: U.S. Department of Commerce.*

2x6 No. 1 Dimension

2x6 No. 2 Dimension

Figure 5. Examples of two available grades of treated dimension lumber.

reducing characteristics visually discernible in that piece. The visual grading rules specifically detail the allowable size and location of knots, the allowable slope of the grain, and other characteristics that affect strength. Additional provisions intended to assure strength, utility, and appearance include specific limits for density, shake, checks, splits, wane, pitch pockets, and other features. For various regions of the country, different grade rule-writing agencies apply NGR criteria to their particular species through published "grading rules."

Grade marks—A grade mark or stamp is placed on dimension lumber to designate the official grade of the piece at the time it was graded. Grade marks are used to inform the dealer of the grade, species or species group, producing mill, moisture content of wood when surfaced, and the grading agency. Grade marks can also be used by the user for assurance of expected quality. Grade marks are applied in ink or are printed on an attached tag. Grade marks should not be confused with preservative treatment quality marks, which will be described later. Some common examples of grade marks are shown in Figure 6. Any remanufacturing of graded lumber, such as ripping, negates the legitimacy of the grade mark. For example, a 10-foot 2 by 6 cut from a 10-foot No. 1 grade 2 by 12 seldom retains the initial grade. Building inspectors look for grade marks when they inspect a structure. If practical, avoid removing the mark when cutting lumber.

Figure 6. Grade marks (stamps) used to designate official grade of lumber and agency logos.

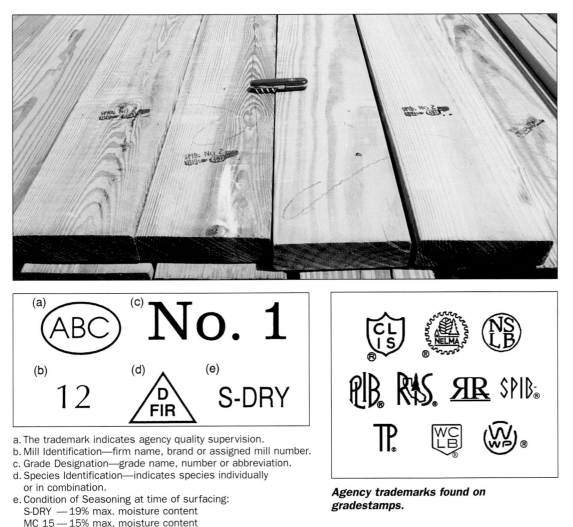

a. The trademark indicates agency quality supervision.
b. Mill Identification—firm name, brand or assigned mill number.
c. Grade Designation—grade name, number or abbreviation.
d. Species Identification—indicates species individually or in combination.
e. Condition of Seasoning at time of surfacing:
   S-DRY — 19% max. moisture content
   MC 15 — 15% max. moisture content
   S-GRN — over 19% moisture content
       (unseasoned)

Agency trademarks found on gradestamps.

Figure 7. Examples of radius edge decking (RED) lumber grades.

Lumber sizes—Commonly available sizes of seasoned and surfaced dimension lumber most often used in decks are given in Table 4. Note that the actual size of the lumber is smaller than the commonly referred to nominal size (2 by 4, 2 by 6, etc.). Although unseasoned and rough (unsurfaced) lumber can also be used, it is not graded and does not have design values. Unseasoned sizes of lumber are also included in Table 4.

Appearance Grades

Some species, such as redwood and cedar, are available in appearance as well as structural grades. Appearance grades generally do not have assigned design values. The factors that affect appearance grades include the presence of heartwood and sapwood; the number, size, and quality of knots; grain orientation; and other natural and manufacturing characteristics.

Decking Lumber Grades

Decking lumber forms the deck surface. Several types of lumber can be used for this purpose, including dimension lumber and radius edge decking (RED) (Fig. 7). RED is available in 1- or 1-1/4-inch thickness (called 5/4 RED). It is typically available in 6-inch widths. Southern pine RED grades are Premium and Standard grades (SPIB). Western species of RED are available in Patio 1 and Patio 2 (WWPA), and Select Dex and Commercial Dex (WCLIB).

Preservative-treated decking lumber may be graded Select Structural, No. 1, or No. 2. The naturally decay-resistant species include redwood and western cedar. Redwood grades include Clear All Heart, Clear, B, Construction Heart, and Construction Common (RIS). Two special-purpose redwood decking grades, Deck Heart and Deck Common, are available for strength as

Table 3. Grade names and physical characteristics of nominal 2x4 dimension lumber produced under American Softwood Lumber Standard.[a]

Grade category	Maximum edge knot (in.)[b]	Wane	Warp (in.)[c]	
			Crook	Twist
Structural Light Framing				
Select Structural	3/4	1/4 thickness, 1/4 width	1/2	9/16
No. 1	1	1/4 thickness, 1/4 width	1/2	9/16
No. 2	1–1/4	1/3 thickness, 1/3 width	11/16	3/4
No. 3	1–3/4	1/2 thickness, 1/2 width	1	1–1/8
Light Framing				
Construction	1–1/2	1/4 thickness, 1/4 width	1/2	9/16
Standard	2	1/3 thickness, 1/3 width	11/16	3/4
Utility	2–1/2	1/2 thickness, 1/2 width	1	1–1/8
Stud				
Stud	1–3/4	1/3 thickness, 1/2 width	3/8	7/16

[a] Source for Table 3: U.S. Department of Commerce 1994.
[b] Larger sizes would have proportionally larger permissible edge knots.
[c] Assuming a 12-foot length, various sizes would have progressively higher or lower limits. Stud grade assumes a 10-foot length.

Table 4. Sizes[a] of surfaced seasoned and unseasoned lumber.

Type and size	Nominal		Actual (dry)		Actual (unseasoned)	
	Thickness	Width	Thickness	Width	Thickness	Width
Radius edge decking						
5/4 x 4	5/4	4	1	3.5	1–1/4	3–9/16
5/4 x 6	5/4	6	1	5.5	1–1/4	5–5/8
Dimension lumber[b]						
2 x 4	2	4	1.5	3.5	1–9/16	3–9/16
2 x 6	2	6	1.5	5.5	1–9/16	5–5/8
2 x 8	2	8	1.5	7.25	1–9/16	7–1/2
2 x 10	2	10	1.5	9.25	1–9/16	9–1/2
2 x 12	2	12	1.5	11.25	1–9/16	11–1/2
4 x 4	4	4	3.5	3.5	3–9/16	3–9/16
4 x 6	4	6	3.5	5.5	3–9/16	5–5/8
4 x 8	4	8	3.5	7.25	3–9/16	7–1/2
Timber[c]						
6 x 6	6	6			5–5/8	5–5/8
6 x 8	6	8			5–5/8	7–1/2
6 x 10	6	10			5–5/8	9–1/2
6 x 12	6	12			5–5/8	11–1/2

[a] All dimensions are in inches.
[b] Least dimension < 5 inches.
[c] Least dimension ≥ 5 inches.

well as appearance. Western redcedar is offered in Architect Clear, Custom Clear, Contractor Clear, Architect Knotty, Custom Knotty, and Contractor Knotty grade categories (WRCLA).

Wood Degradation

Fungi (decay or rot), insects, and weathering are the three primary sources of wood degradation, other than fire. In general, organisms that degrade wood have four basic requirements: moisture, oxygen, adequate temperature, and food. Control of degradation requires the control or alteration of one or more of these requirements. Wood can also undergo slow bacterial degradation in fresh water or be attacked by marine borers in brackish or salt water.

Wood Decay

Wood-degrading fungi are grouped into three categories: brown rot, white rot, and soft rot. Fungi use different wood components as a food source. Some fungi attack the lignin, and others attack the cellulose of wood. As wood-degrading fungi metabolize wood, they decrease wood strength. While this strength loss can vary somewhat depending on the type of fungi involved, it is a rather academic distinction for the deck owner. Brown-rot decay fungi attack the softwood species generally used for decks (Fig. 8). Of importance to the deck owner is the appearance of any mushroom-like fungal fruiting bodies (Fig. 8) which is undoubtedly a sign of advanced decay and serious strength loss. The risk of decay in wood varies considerably throughout the United States (Fig. 9).

Many fungi are classified as mildew (mold) or wood-staining fungi rather than

Figure 8. Fungal decay of wood: (top) wood degraded by brown-rot decay fungi; (bottom) fungal fruiting body (mushroom/toadstool) growing from wood.

wood-degrading fungi because they primarily discolor wood (Fig. 10). Mildew fungi generally do not cause a reduction in strength. These fungi are often a result of poor lumber drying or wet conditions and are objectionable because of their appearance. Because the conditions for these fungi are also favorable for wood-degrading fungal growth, be aware if you observe or suspect mildew growth.

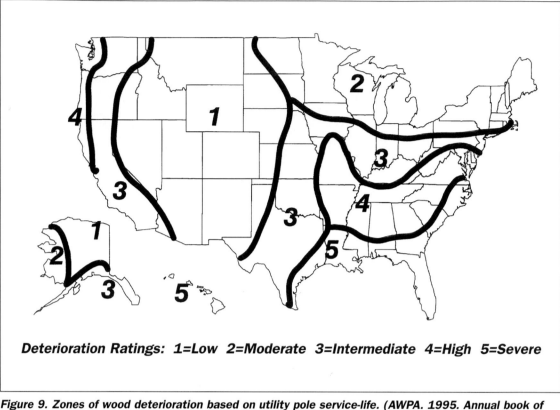

Deterioration Ratings: 1=Low 2=Moderate 3=Intermediate 4=High 5=Severe

Figure 9. Zones of wood deterioration based on utility pole service-life. (AWPA. 1995. Annual book of standards. Woodstock MD: American Wood Preservers' Association.)

The term "dry rot" is often misused to describe wood decay. This term is misleading because the wood, although it may appear to be dry, must have been wet to decay.

Insects

Insects can cause a variety of wood damage, ranging from discoloration of sapwood (caused by fungal growth transported into the wood by insects) to complete degradation. The most common insects associated with wood degradation are termites, beetles, and carpenter ants.

Termites are social insects that live in highly ordered colonies. In the United States, four groups of termites cause degradation of wood in buildings and decks:

Subterranean termites—The most prevalent of the termite groups, subterranean termites are found throughout most of the United States (Fig. 11). Subterranean termites require soil contact and generally attack moist wood. These termites can provide additional moisture to the wood by constructing earthen connecting tubes to wood that is not in contact with the ground.

Formosan termites—Similar to subterranean termites, formosan termites have larger colonies and more aggressive feeding habits. Formosan termites are currently found in the United States along the Gulf Coast and in Hawaii.

Dampwood termites—Similar to subterranean termites, dampwood termites are confined in range to the Pacific Northwest (Fig. 12). These insects require very wet wood and can generally be controlled by removing the moisture source.

Drywood termites—Drywood termites are found in the southwestern United States (Fig. 12). These termites pose the greatest termite-control challenge because

Figure 10. Decay on wood deck: (A) mildew; (B) advanced decay.

they can attack dry wood (as low as 13 percent moisture content). Drywood termites can enter buildings through unscreened air vents and cause extensive damage, leaving little evidence of their activity.

Wood-inhabiting beetles attack wood typically while in the larval stage. Many beetles lay their eggs on the bark of freshly sawn trees, and the larvae continue their development while feeding on the finished wood product. Once they complete their development, they exit the wood and do not reinfest it. Powderpost beetles, however, can attack wood without bark and at moisture contents lower than 20 percent. The larvae of powderpost beetles tunnel throughout the wood, leaving fine wood powder, which gives the beetle its name. High temperatures reached when kiln-drying wood usually destroy the beetle larvae.

Carpenter ants are wood-inhabiting insects that differ from other insects of this type in that they use the wood only for shelter and not for food. Carpenter ants are social insects, much like termites, and construct elaborate galleries only inside decayed wood, particularly large timbers or poles. Carpenter ants are common throughout the eastern United States and Canada, but can be controlled by keeping the wood dry. Ants in wood are good indicators of moisture and decay problems.

Weathering

Weathering is surface degradation of wood caused by sunlight and rain. This degradation causes roughening of the surface, checking and splitting, and wood cell erosion. Erosion (loss of wood cells from the surface) is a slow process, compared to the previously discussed forms of

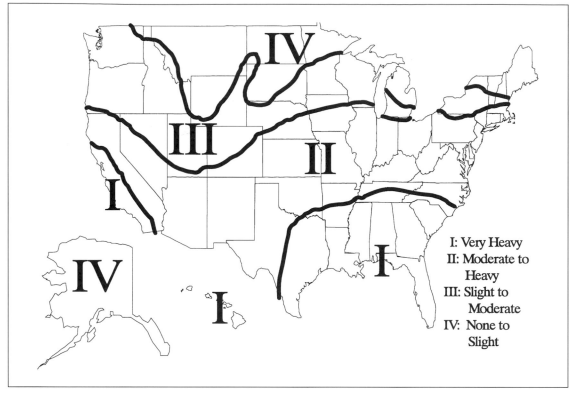

Range map

I: Very Heavy
II: Moderate to
Heavy
III: Slight to
Moderate
IV: None to
Slight

Subterranean termite

Termite tubes

Figure 11. Subterranean termites are found throughout most of the United States.

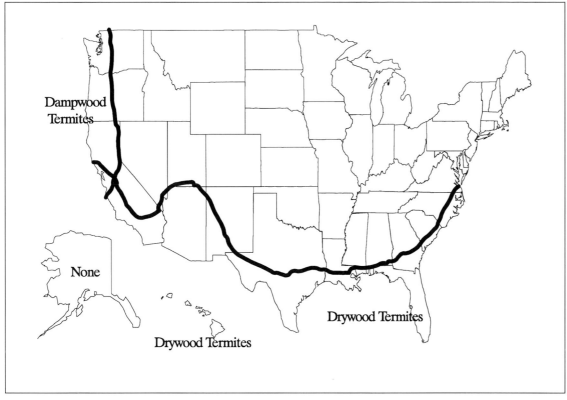

Figure 12. Range of drywood and dampwood termites. (Drawing modified from USDA Termite Center, Gulfport, Mississippi.)

degradation. However, if unprotected, some wood species show considerable weathering effects within a single summer. The weathering process and means to slow its effects are covered in more detail in Chapter 4—Finishing of Decks.

Naturally Decay-Resistant Species

The two most common native species that produce lumber with natural decay resistance are redwood and cedar. The reputation of these species for decay resistance is based on the performance of heartwood cut from large slow-grown trees. The decay resistance of lumber from smaller moderate- to fast-grown trees may not be as great as that of slow-grown timber, particularly if sapwood is present. A few tropical species with natural decay resistance may be available; these species include Ipe (*Tabebuia*-lapacho group), Greenheart (*Ocotea radiaei*), and Bongossi (or Ekki) (*Lophira alata*).

Preservative-Treated Wood: Treatment, Quality Assurance, and Selection

The simplest method for preventing wood decay is to keep wood dry. However, this is not practical for decks or other exposed wood structures. Where temperature, oxygen, and moisture cannot be entirely controlled, the use of decay-resistant wood species and/or wood treated with preservatives are the best options to prevent wood deterioration.

This chapter discusses wood treated with preservatives that are approved by the Environmental Protection Agency (EPA). Typically these preservatives are commercially applied to lumber by pressurized treatment processes before the lumber is sold to the consumer. For outdoor decks and home-improvement projects, the most common preservatives used to treat wood products are chromated copper arsenate (CCA), ammoniacal copper quaternary ammonium chloride (ACQ), and ammoniacal copper zinc arsenate (ACZA) waterborne preservatives.

The preservative chemicals used in commercially available, preservative-treated wood are registered by the EPA as pesticides. These chemicals can be applied to

wood only by a treater with an official Pesticide Applicators License. These chemicals are broad-spectrum pesticides that are introduced into wood under pressure to eliminate the wood as a potential food source for decay fungi and insects.

Preservative Treatments

Preservatives can be applied to the wood either in the factory or in the field (on site), as described in the following.

Factory-Applied Treatments

Preservative treatments are applied to wood in large cylinders under pressure. Lumber is usually treated to standard retention and penetration (that is, the amount of chemical and how deeply it goes into the wood). This treatment meets a specific-use requirement as detailed in the American Wood Preservers' Association standards. These standards require specific penetration limits that, when achieved, allow an untreated core surrounded by a treated shell of wood. In species that have thick sapwood, such as southern pine and ponderosa pine, water can easily move through the sapwood, even after the tree has been harvested

Use and Handling of Preservative-Treated Wood
(Based on EPA/Treating Industry Recommendations)

Consumer Information

Wood treated with an EPA-registered preservative should be used only where protection from insect attack and decay is important.

Waterborne preservatives penetrate deeply into and remain within the treated wood for a long time. Use or exposure to wood treated with waterborne preservatives may present certain hazards. Therefore, the following precautions should be taken both when handling the treated wood and in determining where to use or dispose of the treated wood.

Use-Site Precautions

Wood treated with waterborne preservatives may be used inside residences as long as all sawdust and construction debris are cleaned up and properly disposed of after construction.

Do not use treated wood under circumstances where the preservative may become a component of food or animal feed. Examples of such sites are structures or containers for storing food or silage or for beehives.

Only treated wood that is visibly clean and free of surface residue should be used for patios, decks, and walkways. Treated wood should not be used where it may come into direct or indirect contact with public drinking water, except uses involving incidental contact such as docks and bridges.

Handling Precautions

Dispose of treated wood by ordinary trash collection or burial. Treated wood should not be burned in open fires or in stoves, fireplaces, or residential boilers because toxic chemicals may be produced as part of the smoke and ashes. Treated wood from commercial or industrial sites (e.g., construction sites) may be burned only in commercial incinerators according to State and Federal regulations.

Avoid frequent or prolonged inhalation of sawdust from treated wood. When sawing and machining, wear goggles to protect eyes from flying particles. After working with treated wood, and before eating, drinking, or using tobacco products, wash exposed areas thoroughly. If preservative or sawdust accumulates on clothes, launder the clothes before reuse. Wash work clothes separately from other household clothing.

borne preservative treatments, sufficient chemical can be added to the sapwood to make it possible to protect the wood in high decay-hazard areas, such as in ground contact. The waterborne preservatives CCA and ACQ are used to protect easily-treated woods, like southern pine and ponderosa pine, and moderately difficult-to-treat woods like Hem-Fir.[1] The preservatives ACQ and ACZA are used on woods that are more difficult to treat because the ammonia in the formulation swells the wood to enhance penetration of the preservative. These species include Douglas-fir, which is difficult to treat with CCA.

Other factory-applied preservative treatments include the organic preservatives creosote and oil-borne pentachlorophenol (penta) and copper naphthenate. Organic preservative chemicals are often used for railroad ties and utility poles. These products are not recommended for residential deck construction because of their odor, sometimes tarry surface, and increased chemical leachability.

Field Treatments

The simplest way to apply chemical treatment to wood in a nonfactory or field situation is by brush, soak, or dip treatment. However, it is difficult to achieve adequate preservative penetration by these field-applied methods, and the risk of toxic exposure is greatly increased for individuals doing the treatment and to the environment. As such, field treatments in this section are restricted to discussions of applying water-repellant preservatives (see Types of Finishes in Chapter 4) to field cuts and drilled holes in pressure-treated lumber during construction.

As the term water-repellant implies, water-repellant treatment of end-cuts and drill holes in wood enhances both water repellency and decay resistance of exposed untreated end-grain. This can be especially important because some pressure treatments, when used in aboveground applications, often achieve only a shell of

and cut into lumber. These thick-sapwood species readily accept waterborne preservative treatments, but only in the decay-prone sapwood portion. With water-

---

[1] A marketing group of similar woods which include Western Hemlock, Grand Fir, Noble Fir, White Fir, California Red Fir, and/or Pacific Silver Fir.

treated wood. Water-repellant preservatives alone do not give sufficient decay resistance when used in ground-contact applications.

Wood absorbs liquid water approximately 20 times easier along the grain than across the grain. Because application of water repellant helps retard absorption of liquid water by wood, especially at the end-grain, the wood gets less wet during rainy periods. Although water repellants retard liquid-water absorption by wood, they do little to restrict the movement of water vapor. Thus, the wood dries easily during dry periods, which, in turn, keeps the wood dryer more of the time and minimizes dimensional change. Less dimensional change means less cracking and splitting, less raised grain, and a better looking, longer lasting deck. Water repellant preservatives can be obtained through retail outlets and are intended for use as supplemental wood treatments. These preservatives are discussed more thoroughly in Chapter 4—Finishing of Decks.

Treatment Standards

Preservative-treated wood should have been produced according to American Wood Preservers' Association (AWPA) standards, a series of voluntary standards that describe treating chemicals, processing, quality control, and inspection. Both the AWPA and the American Society for Testing and Materials (ASTM) publish yearly preservative standards. The AWPA treatment standards are used most often.

At the consumer level, the most important information on preservative-treated wood used for decks is the use-category of the preservative. The use-category defines how much preservative chemical is in the wood and how deeply it penetrates into the wood. This is directly correlated to the longevity of the treated wood in exposed environments. Common waterborne preservative use-categories are Above-Ground Use, which has a specified preservative retention of 0.25 lb/ft^3; Ground-Contact Use (0.40 lb/ft^3); and Wood

Foundation and Freshwater Use (0.60 lb/ft^3). When treated and used according to the AWPA standards, treated wood should give decades of service.

Many refractory (that is, difficult-to-treat) wood species require incising. Incising is a process of cutting perforations or slits in the faces and edges of lumber with closely spaced knives. This process greatly increases the penetration of preservative into the wood. Incising lumber before treatment makes it possible to treat wood species that normally could not be treated to acceptable preservative levels. Incising is required by the AWPA and ASTM standards for treatment of thin sapwood species such as Douglas-fir, spruce, hemlock, and fir.

Treatment Quality Assurance

It is impossible to assure proper penetration and retention of preservative by visual inspection. Thus, the only way to assure proper treatment (and long service-life) is to insist that the treated material have an American Lumber Standard Committee (ALSC)-accredited preservative treatment quality mark. The treatment quality mark is the customer's assurance that the wood was treated by a qualified treater and produced under a quality control program audited and sanctioned by an ALSC-accredited, independent, third-party inspection agency (Table 5). The mark designates who treated the wood, the applicable standard to which it was treated, the preservative used, the use-category (i.e., preservative retention level), and the third-party inspection agency. The treatment quality mark can be either a

Table 5. Accredited inspection agencies for waterborne preservative-treated lumber.

Agency	Location
Bode Inspection	Lake Oswego, OR
California Lumber Inspection Service	San Jose, CA
Florida Lumber Inspection Service	Perry, FL
McCutchan Inspection, Inc.	Portland, OR
PFS Corporation	Madison, WI
Southern Pine Inspection Bureau (SPIB)	Pensacola, FL
Timber Products Inspection	Conyers, GA
Warnock Hersey (Canada)	Coquitlam, BC

Accredited by U.S. Department of Commerce, American Lumber Standards Committee.

second ink mark in addition to the grade mark or a plastic tag stapled to one end of the lumber (Figs. 13 and 14). The treatment quality mark designates the use-category of the preservative treatment and assures its quality. If a treater fails to maintain the treatment level designated in the standards, the use of the treatment quality mark is revoked. **The treatment quality mark is the consumer's only assurance of the quality of the treatment.** As such, it is illegal to fraudulently use or alter the treatment quality mark before construction.

Preservative-treated lumber that has only a treater guarantee is also available. This lumber usually has a plastic tag stapled to the end of each piece that does not specifically designate any ALSC-accredited third-party inspection agency. Be aware that lumber with only a treater tag will not have been inspected by an independent inspection agency and does not meet the requirements for the major model building codes, HUD, FHA/VA, and other Federal agencies such as the Department of Defense. The guarantee is backed only by the treater. The consumer is advised to read "the fine print," which typically says that the piece is guaranteed for a specific length of time (often 30 to 40 years). If, however, the piece decays within that period, it will be replaced by the treater. Associated costs of reconstruction are usually not covered. Occasionally, lumber will have both a treatment quality mark and a treater tag.

In spite of these quality control efforts, some treated lumber on the market does not have preservative treatment quality marks. This lumber often carries no guarantee and might not be treated according to any standard. It looks identical in color to the quality-marked lumber but may not have enough preservative chemical retention or penetration to provide long-term protection against decay or termites.

Post-Treatment Drying

Waterborne preservative treatment raises the moisture content of wood to a level above its fiber saturation point (i.e., the wood is soaking wet). Occasionally, wood is re-dried after treatment. The following text describes kiln-drying in the factory and ways to dry treated wood yourself.

Use of Wet Wood

Wood will eventually dry to an equilibrium moisture content that depends on relative humidity and temperature of the surrounding environment. For many areas of the country, this is about 12 percent moisture. It will dry to this moisture content either before the deck is constructed (if stickered and adequate time is allowed, usually 2 to 3 summer months) or after the deck is constructed. It is best if the wood dries before the deck is constructed. Techniques for air drying lumber are outlined in the Do-It-Yourself Drying section (page 23).

The use of undried wood (wood above its fiber saturation point) in deck construction can lead to several problems caused by the shrinkage of the wood. Mitered corners, particularly those at the corner of railings, can shrink unevenly. Uneven shrinkage in length can also occur; however, this usually only happens to pith-containing lumber with a high proportion of juvenile wood.

Shrinkage of decking boards is also a problem. Normally, after the decking boards are installed, a line is snapped along the end of the deck and all the boards are crosscut to produce an even edge to the deck. As these boards dry, uneven longitudinal shrinkage of the decking boards can result in an uneven edge. In extreme cases involving juvenile wood, the fasteners may pull out (see Fig. 3). Tangential shrinkage may also cause uneven spacing of the decking boards.

An advantage to using wet, treated wood is that it is much easier to nail or screw than dry wood, and the deck can be built immediately.

ABC [1]

XXX [7]

19_-19_ [3]
GROUND CONTACT [6]
.40 [5]

AWPA ___ STDS [2]
PRESERVATIVE [4]
KDAT [8]
X-XX [9]

1. The identifying symbol, logo, or name of the accredited agency.
2. The applicable American Wood Preservers' Association (AWPA) commodity standard.
3. The year of treatment if required by AWPA standard.
4. The preservative used, which may be abbreviated.
5. The preservative retention.
6. The exposure category (e.g. Above Ground, Ground Contact, etc.).
7. The plant name and location; or plant name and number; or plant number.
8. If applicable, moisture content after treatment.
9. If applicable, length, and/or class.

Figure 13. Hypothetical example of a treatment quality mark accredited by the U.S. Department of Commerce American Lumber Standard Committee for marking lumber treated with waterborne preservatives.

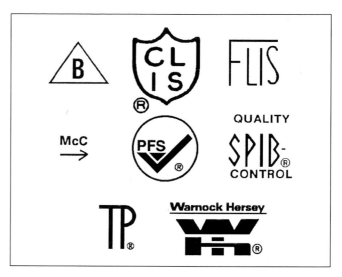

Figure 14. Examples of ALSC-accredited inspection agency logos found on treatment quality marks for lumber treated with waterborne preservatives.

Factory Drying

Unless the material is marked (Fig. 13) as kiln-dried after treatment (KDAT) or air-dried after treatment (ADAT), treated lumber is usually only drip-dried before banding for shipment. Lumber at the retail lumber yard sometimes appears dry on the surface. However, the lumber is still very wet inside (moisture content greater than 50 percent).

When wet preservative-treated wood dries without restraint, it can warp (Fig. 15). This can be minimized by covering the lumber pile to restrict drying until it is "nailed down." Once properly fastened in place, the lumber will still shrink as it dries, but excessive twisting and warping can usually be minimized.

Drying decreases the handling hazard, weight, and shrinkage of treated wood. It is recommended that you buy treated lumber that has been air-dried or kiln-dried after treatment or that you air-dry the wet, treated lumber yourself before use.

Do-It-Yourself Drying

If KDAT lumber is not available, undried treated lumber can be air dried before use. It is best if the lumber can be stickered and piled under cover on a solid base several inches above ground, with the pile sides open for good air movement. Figure 16 shows the 3/4-inch-thick stickers used to permit air movement between layers of lumber. To keep the top pieces from warping, it is necessary to place weight on the stickered and covered stacks of lumber. Note that the stickers between layers are aligned vertically. This distributes the weight of the wood directly on each sticker. If the stickers are not aligned, the lumber will bend and dry with a permanent warp. Stickers should be placed about every 2 feet. In extremely dry areas of the country, the ends of lumber are prone to split during drying because they dry more rapidly than the rest of the piece. This can be avoided by sealing the end-grain after the lumber is stacked. If the end-grain of the lumber will

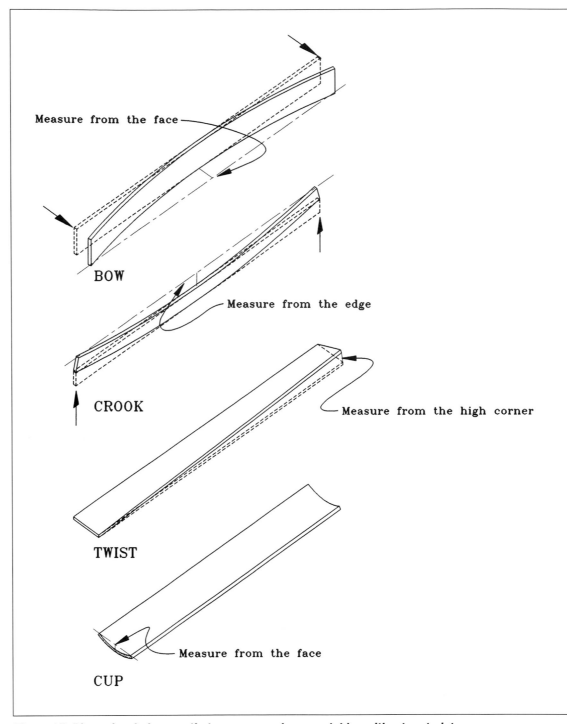

Figure 15. Dimensional changes that can occur when wood dries without restraint.

show after construction, some care is necessary in choosing the end-grain sealer.

End-grain can be sealed with oil-based primer paint, varnish, or melted paraffin wax. This end-grain treatment will somewhat increase the drying time, but it will decrease splitting.

The amount of time needed to dry lumber depends on the species, thickness, and weather conditions (temperature and relative humidity). At least 2 months of summer weather are needed for 1-1/2-inch-thick lumber to air dry. Increasing air movement through the stack by using a fan can

Figure 16. Suggested method of stickering and stacking lumber for air drying.

cut air-drying time to about 1 month. You can use the weight of the wood to check the dryness of the lumber. At the beginning of the project, preweigh several pieces of the lumber; check their weight again after a couple of weeks. When the wood is ready to use, its weight should be about 2/3 the original weight. A bathroom scale is adequate for determining the weight loss of the wood.

Selection of Treated Lumber

Grades selected for a deck depend on design, cost, and local building codes. Not all grades are available everywhere, and selection of alternative grades may be necessary.

Choose a deck design that will satisfy the local building codes and consider the decay and termite hazard in your area. Find a lumberyard familiar with how softwood lumber is graded, how it is treated, how to read ALSC-accredited grade marks and treatment quality marks, and how to identify heartwood and sapwood. Be aware of the potential for warpage problems with juvenile wood and flat-grained lumber.

Here are some suggestions for selecting lumber. Spend some time comparing the quality and price of lumber at various lumberyards. Ask for sales catalogs. Look at how the lumber is stored. Check the quality mark to see if the treated wood was kiln-dried after treatment (KDAT). Kiln-dried lumber should be stored inside or at least under pro-

tective cover. Check for water stains or other indications of previous exposure to water.

Many retail lumber yards offer help and may even provide deck design services. The design may take the form of computer-generated drawings, complete with a list of all the materials needed for construction. Some lumberyards offer discounts for large purchases. Talk to your supplier, but do not assume that all lumberyard employees know more about lumber quality, treatments and treatment quality, or wood deck construction than you do.

The dimensional stability of different wood species is affected by the width and density differences between early- and latewood growth-ring bands. For example, in species having wide, dense latewood bands and low-density earlywood bands, the differential shrinking and swelling of the bands with changes in moisture content can cause large stresses in the wood that can result in raised grain and shelling. Raised grain is most severe on flat-grained lumber. Shelling is an extreme case of raised grain in which the latewood bands separate from the earlywood bands to form a knifelike or spearlike edge (Fig. 4). This is one reason why deck lumber is often recommended to be placed pith-side down (or bark-side up). If the two sides of a particular board are of equal quality, it is best to place the board bark-side up. If, however, the pith-side is clearly the better side, place this side up.

Photo courtesy of the Southern Forest Products Association, Southern Pine Marketing Council.

Photo courtesy of the Southern Forest Products Association, Southern Pine Marketing Council.

Photo courtesy of Western Wood Products Association.

Photo courtesy of Western Wood Products Association.

3

▲ ▲ ▲ ▲ ▲ ▲ ▲ ▲ ▲ ▲ ▲ ▲ ▲ ▲ ▲ ▲ ▲ ▲

STRUCTURAL DESIGN AND CONSTRUCTION OF DECKS

The performance of the deck as a structural system is one of the most important considerations in building a wood deck. The structure of a deck is not unlike the skeleton of a conventionally framed wood house, minus the sheathing, siding, and roof that provide structural stability and protection from the environment. Fully exposed to the degrading effects of the weather, the structural members of a deck must be properly designed and connected to assure long-term, safe performance.

The structural support of a deck comes from the proper sizing, placement, and connection of posts, beams, joists, and decking boards. This chapter provides information on how to properly size these components, and how to choose the appropriate fasteners to join them. The final decision should be checked and approved by a design professional and/or building official.

Deck Structure

Local building codes typically provide the minimum design requirements for wood decks. For cases where specific designs are not provided, span tables for structural members based upon the dead and live load requirements typically used for houses and other structures are offered. Live loads include the weights of people, nonstationary furniture, and other nonpermanent loads. Dead loads include the weight of the deck itself, railings, benches, fixed planters, and other permanent objects. The allowable spans for two live load levels of 40 lb/ft^2 and 60 lb/ft^2, with a 10 lb/ft^2 dead load, are provided.

The allowable spans for decking, joists, and beams and the sizing of posts depend on the species, grade, size, and spacing of the members. In this section, allowable spans are given for the various deck components. The spans were determined on the basis of accepted wood engineering design criteria and allowable design properties for various wood species and grades given in the National Design Specifications for Wood Construction (NDS)[1]. These spans have been determined on the basis of allowable stresses and deflections assuming simple spans in a structurally stable struc-

---

[1] ANSI/NFPA 1991. Design values for wood construction. National Design Specification. Washington, DC: National Forest Products Association (now American Forest and Paper Association [AF&PA]).

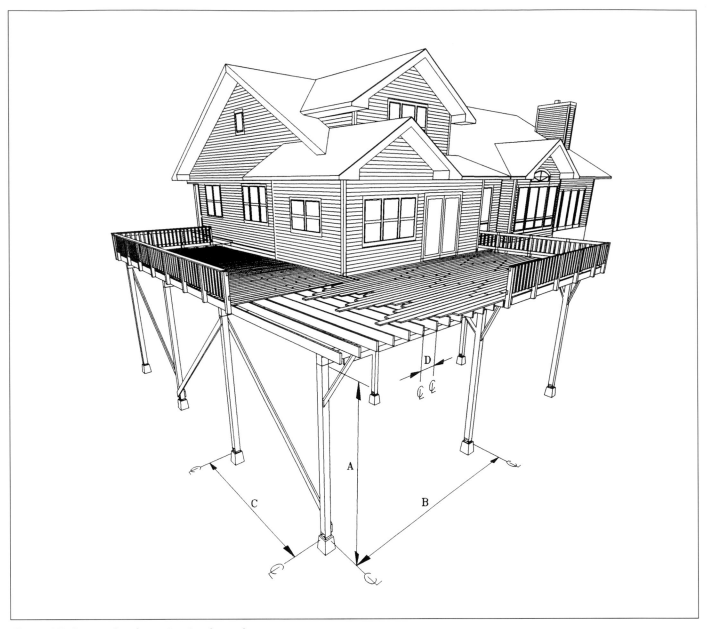

Figure 17. Spans of various structural members.

ture and were developed in cooperation with several wood products associations (see Acknowledgements).

Although these allowable spans are equally applicable for decks built at ground level or those that are elevated, it is important that the deck designer realize the importance of deck stability, especially for elevated decks. Because the consequences of failure for an elevated deck are obviously much more severe than that for a ground level deck, the deck designer should pay particular attention to the recommendations given for deck bracing and deck attachment to the house, which provide the structural stability necessary for elevated decks.

Span Tables for Framing Decks

Although the arrangement of the structural members in a deck can vary somewhat based on such factors as the orientation of the deck, position of the house, and shape of the lot, the basic structural system is generally the same. The decking boards are supported by the joists, which rest on the beams, which in turn are supported by the posts. The posts are connected to a foundation (footing) and transfer the loads from the deck structure to the ground. Figure 17 shows this typical structural arrangement. This chapter provides tables for determining the proper spacing and size of the structural members of a deck. For design convenience, the span tables (Tables 8 through 13) are divided into species groups on the basis of similar engineering strength and stiffness properties given in the NDS[1]. One group includes Douglas Fir and Southern Pine; a second group, Hem-Fir, Spruce-Pine-Fir (SPF), and SPF (south); and a third group, Western Cedar, Redwood, and Ponderosa Pine. The specific species designations (i.e., SPF (south), Redwood) refer to those given in the NDS[1]. To assure adequate structural designs for high moisture conditions, wet-use condition factors were used in computing allowable spans. The use of these factors result in designs that are somewhat conservative in dry environments. **The tables assume the structural lumber used as a grade of No. 2 and Better.** Member size and spans are those which would be typical for most residential decks.

If unusual loading conditions are anticipated (such as when heavy planters or hot tubs are to be supported by the deck), consultation with a structural engineer or other design professional knowledgeable in wood engineering design is advised. Throughout this chapter, reference is made to nominal lumber sizes, not actual lumber sizes (i.e., 2 by 6 inches, not 1-1/2 by 5-1/2 inches) (see Table 4).

Post Sizes

The most common sizes of posts used for residential deck construction are 4x4 and 6x6, although 4x6 posts can be used (see Table 4 for dimensions). The necessary size of the post is usually determined from the area of deck it supports, the deck load, and the post height; though architectural aesthetics may also play a role. The allowable heights of posts for various post sizes supporting a given tributary load area are listed in Tables 6 and 7 for 40 and 60 lb/ft[2] loading, respectively. The post height is the distance from the footing to the post attachment to the beam. This is shown as dimension A in Figure 17.

In most cases, the load area supported by a post (called the tributary load area) needs to be calculated to determine the appropriate post size. This load area is most often found by multiplying the beam spacing by the post spacing; perimeter posts typically support half as much area. Figure 18 shows tributary load areas (shaded) of various posts in a typical deck. For uniformity in detailing and construction, it is usually prudent to determine which post in the deck has the largest load area and/or the greatest required height, and then select the same size of post for the whole deck. For nontypical or nonsymmetrical deck layouts, tributary load areas may need to be computed for individual posts.

From an architectural point of view, it is often desirable to use a post of greater dimension than may be required structurally because larger posts give the deck a more solid look. Tall 4x4 posts can look spindly, and any warping that occurs is accentuated by the smaller dimension. As will be discussed later, posts of long unsupported height require bracing to assure adequate stability for the deck.

Beam Spans

The allowable beam span is based upon the cross-sectional size of the beam and the tributary load it supports. The beam span is the distance between the posts upon which the beam rests (dimension B in Figs. 17 and 18). The tributary load is calculated based on a "tributary load width" carried by the beam. For larger decks, the tributary load width is determined as the spacing between a beam and any adjacent beams, and may or may not include the area of deck overhang, as shown in Figure 19 (A and B). For smaller decks (with only two beams or a beam and attachment to the house), the tributary load width is as shown in Figure 19 (C and D). A calculation of these tributary load widths is necessary to properly size deck beams for various spans, which are given in Tables 8 through 13. Several commonly available beam sizes are shown.

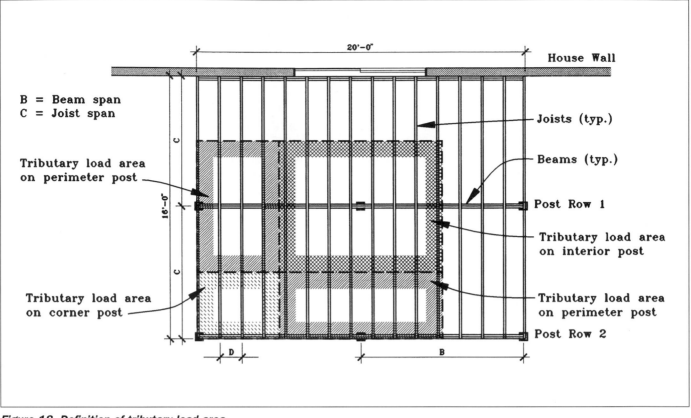

Figure 18. Definition of tributary load area.

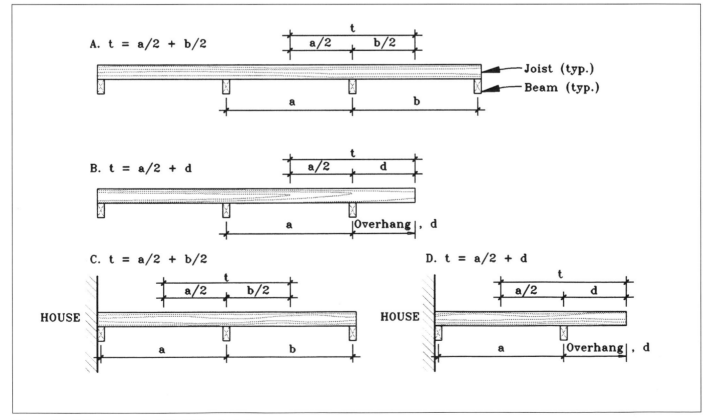

Figure 19. Tributary load width (t) for deck beams.

Table 6. Maximum post heights for 40 lb/ft² deck design.

Species	Post size	40 lb/ft² deck design Tributary load area to post (ft²)																		
		36	48	60	72	84	96	108	120	132	144	156	168	180	192	204	216	228	240	256
Southern pine, Douglas-fir	4x4	10'	10'	10'	9'	9'	8'	8'	7'	7'	6'	6'	6'	6'	5'	5'	5'	4'	4'	4'
	4x6	14'	14'	13'	12'	11'	10'	10'	9'	9'	8'	8'	8'	7'	7'	7'	7'	6'	6'	6'
	6x6 (No.1)	17'	17'	17'	17'	17'	17'	17'	17'	17'	17'	17'	17'	16'	16'	15'	15'	14'	14'	13'
	6x6 (No.2)	17'	17'	17'	17'	17'	17'	17'	17'	16'	16'	15'	14'	13'	13'	12'	11'	10'	8'	
Hem-Fir, SPF	4x4	10'	10'	10'	9'	9'	8'	8'	7'	7'	6'	6'	6'	6'	5'	5'	5'	4'	4'	4'
	4x6	14'	14'	13'	12'	11'	11'	10'	9'	9'	9'	8'	8'	8'	7'	7'	7'	7'	6'	6'
	6x6 (No.1)	17'	17'	17'	17'	17'	17'	17'	17'	17'	17'	17'	16'	16'	15'	15'	14'	13'	13'	12'
	6x6 (No.2)	17'	17'	17'	17'	17'	17'	17'	17'	16'	15'	13'	12'	10'	8'					
Ponderosa pine, Redwood, Western cedar, SPF (south)	4x4	10'	10'	9'	8'	7'	7'	6'	6'	5'	4'									
	4x6	14'	13'	12'	11'	10'	9'	8'	8'	7'	7'	7'	6'	6'	5'	5'	4'	4'		
	6x6 (No.1)	17'	17'	17'	17'	17'	17'	17'	17'	16'	15'	15'	14'	14'	13'	13'	12'	12'	11'	11'
	6x6 (No.2)	17'	17'	17'	17'	17'	16'	13'	7'											

Table 6 used with permission from American Forest and Paper Association. Live load in pounds per square foot; 10 lb/ft² dead load also included.

Table 7. Maximum post heights for 60 lb/ft² deck design.

Species	Post size	60 lb/ft² deck design Tributary load area to post (ft²)																		
		36	48	60	72	84	96	108	120	132	144	156	168	180	192	204	216	228	240	256
Southern pine, Douglas-fir	4x4	10'	10'	9'	8'	7'	7'	6'	6'	5'	5'	5'								
	4x6	14'	12'	11'	10'	9'	9'	8'	8'	7'	7'	7'	6'	6'	6'	5'	5'	5'	5'	
	6x6 (No.1)	17'	17'	17'	17'	17'	17'	17'	17'	16'	15'	14'	14'	13'	13'	12'	12'	11'	11'	10'
	6x6 (No.2)	17'	17'	17'	17'	17'	16'	15'	14'	13'	12'	11'	9'	6'						
Hem-Fir, SPF	4x4	10'	10'	9'	8'	7'	7'	6'	6'	6'	5'	5'								
	4x6	14'	13'	11'	10'	9'	9'	8'	8'	7'	7'	7'	6'	6'	6'	5'	5'			
	6x6 (No.1)	17'	17'	17'	17'	17'	17'	17'	16'	16'	15'	14'	13'	12'	12'	11'	10'	9'	8'	7'
	6x6 (No.2)	17'	17'	17'	17'	17'	16'	14'	12'	10'										
Ponderosa pine, Redwood, Western cedar, SPF (south)	4x4	10'	9'	7'	7'	6'	5'													
	4x6	13'	11'	10'	9'	8'	7'	7'	6'	5'	5'									
	6x6 (No.1)	17'	17'	17'	17'	17'	16'	15'	14'	13'	13'	12'	11'	11'	10'	10'	9'	9'	8'	6'
	6x6 (No.2)	17'	17'	17'	15'	9'														

Table 7 used with permission from American Forest and Paper Association. Live load in pounds per square foot; 10 lb/ft² dead load also included.

Table 8. Maximum beam spans for Douglas-fir and Southern pine for 40 lb/ft² design load.

Beam size	**40 lb/ft² design load** Douglas-fir, Southern pine												
	Tributary load width (ft)												
	4'	5'	6'	7'	8'	9'	10'	11'	12'	13'	14'	15'	16'
(2) 2x6	7'	6'											
(2) 2x8	9'	8'	7'	7'	6'	6'							
(2) 2x10	11'	10'	9'	8'	8'	7'	7'	6'	6'	6'	6'		
(3) 2x8	12'	11'	10'	9'	8'	8'	7'	7'	7'	6'	6'	6'	
(2) 2x12	13'	12'	10'	10'	9'	8'	8'	7'	7'	7'	6'	6'	6'
(3) 2x10	15'	13'	12'	11'	10'	10'	9'	9'	8'	8'	8'	7'	7'
(3) 2x12	16'	15'	14'	13'	12'	11'	11'	10'	10'	9'	9'	8'	8'
4x6	7'	7'	6'										
4x8	10'	9'	8'	7'	7'	6'	6'	6'					
6x8	12'	10'	9'	9'	8'	8'	7'	7'	6'	6'	6'	6'	
4x10	12'	11'	10'	9'	8'	8'	7'	7'	7'	6'	6'	6'	6'
4x12	14'	13'	11'	10'	10'	9'	9'	8'	8'	7'	7'	7'	7'
6x10	15'	13'	12'	11'	10'	10'	9'	9'	8'	8'	7'	7'	7'
6x12	16'	16'	15'	13'	12'	12'	11'	10'	10'	10'	9'	9'	8'

Tables 8-13 used with permission from American Forest and Paper Association. Spans are distances in feet between posts or support. Grade is No. 2 or Better. Number in parentheses is number of full-length nailed laminations. Live load in pounds per square foot; 10 lb/ft² dead load included in span calculation. See Figure 19 for definition of tributary load width.

Beam size	**40 lb/ft² design load** Hem-Fir, SPF, SPF (south)												
	Tributary load width (ft)												
	4'	5'	6'	7'	8'	9'	10'	11'	12'	13'	14'	15'	16'
(2) 2x6	6'	6'											
(2) 2x8	8'	7'	6'	6'									
(2) 2x10	10'	9'	8'	7'	7'	6'	6'						
(3) 2x8	11'	10'	9'	8'	7'	7'	6'	6'	6'				
(2) 2x12	11'	10'	9'	8'	8'	7'	7'	6'	6'	6'			
(3) 2x10	13'	12'	11'	10'	9'	8'	8'	8'	7'	7'	6'	6'	
(3) 2x12	15'	14'	12'	11'	11'	10'	9'	9'	8'	8'	8'	7'	7'
4x6	7'	6'	6'										
4x8	9'	8'	7'	6'	6'	6'							
6x8	9'	8'	8'	7'	7'	6'	6'	6'					
4x10	11'	10'	9'	8'	7'	7'	6'	6'	6'				
4x12	13'	11'	10'	9'	9'	8'	7'	7'	7'	6'	6'	6'	
6x10	12'	11'	10'	9'	8'	8'	7'	7'	7'	6'	6'	6'	6'
6x12	15'	13'	12'	11'	10'	10'	9'	9'	8'	8'	7'	7'	7'

Table 9. Maximum beam spans for Hem-Fir, SPF, and SPF (south) for 40 lb/ft² design load.

40 lb/ft² design load
Ponderosa pine, Redwood, Western cedar

Beam size	Tributary load width (ft)												
	4'	5'	6'	7'	8'	9'	10'	11'	12'	13'	14'	15'	16'
(2) 2x6	6'												
(2) 2x8	8'	7'	6'	6'									
(2) 2x10	9'	8'	8'	7'	6'	6'	6'						
(3) 2x8	10'	9'	8'	8'	7'	7'	6'	6'					
(2) 2x12	11'	10'	9'	8'	7'	7'	7'	6'	6'				
(3) 2x10	13'	11'	10'	9'	8'	8'	7'	7'	7'				
(3) 2x12	15'	13'	12'	11'	10'	9'	9'	8'	8'	8'	7'	7'	7'
4x6	7'	6'											
4x8	8'	7'	7'	6'	6'								
6x8	9'	8'	8'	7'	6'	6'	6'						
4x10	10'	9'	8'	8'	7'	7'	6'	6'	6'				
4x12	12'	11'	10'	9'	8'	8'	7'	7'	6'	6'	6'	6'	
6x10	12'	11'	10'	9'	8'	8'	7'	7'	7'	6'	6'	6'	
6x12	15'	13'	12'	11'	10'	9'	9'	8'	8'	8'	7'	7'	7'

Table 10. Maximum beam spans for Ponderosa pine, Redwood, and Western cedar for 40 lb/ft² design load.

Tables 8-13 used with permission from American Forest and Paper Association. Spans are distances in feet between posts or support. Grade is No. 2 or Better. Number in parentheses is number of full-length nailed laminations. Live load in pounds per square foot; 10 lb/ft² dead load included in span calculation. See Figure 19 for definition of tributary load width.

Table 11. Maximum beam spans for Douglas-fir and Southern pine for 60 lb/ft² design load.

60 lb/ft² design load
Douglas-fir, Southern pine

Beam size	Tributary load width (ft)												
	4'	5'	6'	7'	8'	9'	10'	11'	12'	13'	14'	15'	16'
(2) 2x6	6'												
(2) 2x8	7'	7'	6'										
(2) 2x10	9'	8'	7'	7'	6'								
(3) 2x8	10'	9'	8'	7'	7'	6'	6'						
(2) 2x12	11'	10'	9'	8'	7'	7'	6'	6'	6'				
(3) 2x10	12'	11'	10'	9'	9'	8'	8'	7'	7'	6'	6'	6'	6'
(3) 2x12	14'	13'	12'	11'	10'	9'	9'	8'	8'	8'	7'	7'	6'
4x6	6'												
4x8	8'	7'	6'	6'									
6x8	10'	9'	8'	7'	7'	6'	6'						
4x10	10'	9'	8'	7'	7'	6'	6'	6'					
4x12	12'	10'	9'	9'	8'	8'	7'	7'	6'	6'	6'		
6x10	12'	11'	10'	9'	9'	8'	8'	7'	7'	6'	6'	6'	6'
6x12	15'	13'	12'	11'	10'	10'	9'	9'	8'	8'	8'	7'	7'

Table 12. Maximum beam spans for Hem-Fir, SPF, and SPF (south) for 60 lb/ft² design load.

60 lb/ft² design load
Hem-Fir, SPF, SPF (south)

Beam size	Tributary load width (ft)												
	4'	5'	6'	7'	8'	9'	10'	11'	12'	13'	14'	15'	16'
(2) 2x6	5'												
(2) 2x8	7'	6'											
(2) 2x10	8'	7'	7'	6'									
(3) 2x8	9'	8'	7'	7'	6'								
(2) 2x12	10'	9'	8'	7'	6'	6'							
(3) 2x10	11'	10'	9'	8'	8'	7'	6'	6'					
(3) 2x12	13'	11'	10'	9'	9'	8'	8'	7'	6'	6'	6'		
4x6	6'												
4x8	7'	7'	6'										
6x8	8'	7'	6'	6'									
4x10	9'	8'	7'	7'	6'								
4x12	10'	9'	8'	8'	7'	7'	6'	6'					
6x10	10'	9'	8'	8'	7'	7'	6'	6'	6'				
6x12	12'	11'	10'	9'	9'	8'	8'	7'	6'	6'	6'	6'	6'

Tables 8-13 used with permission from American Forest and Paper Association. Spans are distances in feet between posts or support. Grade is No. 2 or Better. Number in parentheses is number of full-length nailed laminations. Live load in pounds per square foot; 10 lb/ft² dead load included in span calculation. See Figure 19 for definition of tributary load width.

60 lb/ft² design load
Ponderosa pine, Redwood, Western cedar

Beam size	Tributary load width (ft)												
	4'	5'	6'	7'	8'	9'	10'	11'	12'	13'	14'	15'	16'
(2) 2x8	6'	6'											
(2) 2x10	8'	7'	6'	6'									
(3) 2x8	9'	8'	7'	6'	6'								
(2) 2x12	9'	8'	7'	7'	6'	6'							
(3) 2x10	11'	9'	8'	8'	7'	7'	6'	6'					
(3) 2x12	12'	11'	10'	9'	8'	8'	7'	7'	6'	6'			
4x8	7'	6'	6'										
6x8	8'	7'	6'	6'									
4x10	9'	8'	7'	6'									
4x12	10'	9'	8'	7'	7'	6'	6'						
6x10	10'	9'	8'	7'	7'	6'	6'	6'					
6x12	12'	11'	10'	9'	8'	8'	7'	7'	7'	6'	6'	6'	

Table 13. Maximum beam spans for Ponderosa pine, Redwood, and Western cedar for 60 lb/ft² design load.

Because it is often convenient to nail together dimensional lumber into beams of larger cross-section, some of these common sizes are included in the tables as well. If these built-up beams are to be used, remember that **the individual pieces of lumber must be the same length as the beam to be manufactured,** for the values in Tables 8 through 13 to be applicable. In other words, the values in the tables do **not** allow for butt joints occurring in the beam span. An alternating top and bottom nail pattern, as shown in Figure 20 is recommended to join the individual lumber pieces together. Be sure to use nails that are properly coated or corrosion-proof and of sufficient length to fully penetrate at least two members (see section on Fasteners, page 39). Where practical, the dimension of the post should be the same as the beam width to simplify fastening the post and beam together. For example, a 4x8 beam (on edge) is best matched with a 4x4 or 4x6 post.

Joist Spans

The joist span is the distance between the beams (dimension C in Figs. 17 and 18). The allowable span of 2 by x joists is determined by the joist spacing and the depth (x) of the joist. The most common

sizes of joists are 2x6, 2x8, 2x10, and 2x12. Table 14 lists the allowable spans for deck joists of these common sizes for the two loadings and the different species groups. Note that joist spacings of 12, 16, and 24 inches are provided. These are the most common joist spacings and are compatible with the allowable spans of commonly available decking boards. Although shown in the joist span tables, 2x12 joists are not always readily available in some species.

Decking Board Spans

Traditionally, 2x4 and 2x6 structural lumber has been used for decking boards. Although these lumber sizes are still used for decking, 5/4 radius edge decking (RED) is becoming more popular. One advantage to RED is that the edges are rounded, which reduces the occurrence of splinters and makes the wood look less massive. In any case, the use of decking boards wider than 6 inches is **not** recommended because cup, a form of warp, can become a problem.

Allowable spans for 2x4, 2x6, and radius edge (4/4 and 5/4) decking for the various species are given in Table 15 (see dimension D in Figs. 17 and 18). Reduce the allowable decking spans if the decking is applied diagonally (e.g., 24 to 16, 16 to 12).

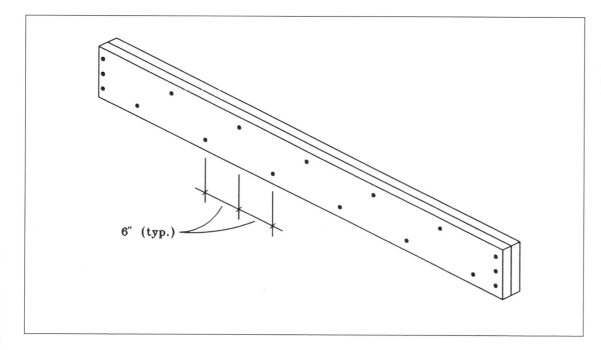

Figure 20. Nailing pattern for nail-laminated beams.

6" (typ.)

Table 14. Maximum joist spans.

Species	Joist Size	Joist Spacing (inches on center)					
		40 lb/ft²			60 lb/ft²		
		12"	16"	24"	12"	16"	24"
Douglas–fir, Southern pine	2x6	10'4"	9'5"	7'10"	9'0"	8'2"	6'8"
	2x8	13'8"	12'5"	10'2"	11'11"	10'6"	8'7"
	2x10	17'5"	15'5"	12'7"	15'0"	13'0"	10'7"
	2x12	20'0"	17'10"	14'7"	17'5"	15'1"	12'4"
Hem–Fir, SPF, SPF (south)	2x6	9'2"	8'4"	7'3"	8'0"	7'3"	6'3"
	2x8	12'1"	10'11"	9'6"	10'6"	9'6"	8'0"
	2x10	15'4"	14'0"	11'7"	13'5"	12'0"	9'10"
	2x12	18'8"	16'6"	13'6"	16'1"	14'0"	10'10"
Ponderosa pine, Redwood, Western cedar	2x6	8'10"	8'0"	7'0"	7'9"	7'0"	5'11"
	2x8	11'8"	10'7"	8'10"	10'2"	9'2"	7'6"
	2x10	14'10"	13'3"	10'10"	12'11"	11'2"	9'2"
	2x12	17'9"	15'4"	12'7"	15'0"	13'0"	10'7"

Table 14 used with permission from the American Forest and Paper Association. Spans are distances between posts or support. Grade is No. 2 or Better. Based upon 1/360 deflection limitation. Joists are on edge. Spans are distances between beams or support. Live load in pounds per square foot; 10 lb/ft² dead load included in span calculation.

Example of Structural Member Sizing

The following example further illustrates the use of the described design tables. Suppose the structural members of a deck are designed for a 40-lb/ft² live load. To accommodate deck access from a second-story master bedroom, a post height of 8 feet is assumed (dimension A in Fig. 17). Assume a 16 x 20 foot plan is chosen from a preliminary design and will have the layout shown in Figure 18. The joists are assumed to run perpendicular to the house and beams will support the joists on two rows of posts (labeled Post Row 1 and Post Row 2 in Fig. 18). Assume that preservative-treated Southern Pine is to be used for the structural lumber (posts, beams, and joists) and redwood is chosen for the decking.

Post Design—As Figure 18 shows, the post carrying the largest tributary load area is at the center of the deck. The loaded area that this post must support is equal to the shaded area around the interior post. This tributary load area is equal to 80 ft² (10 feet times 8 feet), since this post carries a load half the distance to the next post in both directions. Table 6 shows that a Southern Pine 4x4 post 8 feet high will support a tributary load area of 108 ft². Note that a 4x6 Southern Pine post will support a tributary load area of 168 ft². Both exceed the 80 ft² required. The 4x4 is selected for economy.

Beam Design—The layout of Figure 18 shows that the beams supporting the joists will span 10 feet, the distance between the posts along the long deck dimension (dimension B in Fig. 18). The tributary load width, t, for the beams along Post Row 1 is found from Figure 19, C and is computed as 8 feet (t = a/2 + b/2 = 8 ft/2 + 8 ft/2 = 8 feet, or half the deck span on both sides of the beam). From Table 8, it is seen that beams made from three nail-laminated 2x10's will span the required 10 feet (at a beam tributary load width of 8 feet). Moving vertically down the table, it is seen that a 4x12 or a 6x10 could also be selected to span the 10 feet (at a tributary load width of 8 feet).

The beams that span along Post Row 2 carry only half the tributary load of the beams of Post Row 1. The tributary load width, t, for these beams can be determined from Figure 19, B. Because no overhang is considered in this design, d = 0 in Figure 19, B. Therefore, t = a/2 + d = 8 ft/2 + 0 = 4 feet for the beams of Post Row 2. Again referring to Table 8, it is seen that beams made from two nail-laminated 2x10's will span 11 feet (at a beam tributary load width of 4 feet), greater than the 10 feet required. Again moving vertically down Table 8, it is seen that a 4x8 will also span the 10 feet at a tributary load width of 4 feet.

Joist Design—To determine the proper joist size to span between the beams, Table 14 is consulted. Assuming the joists will be spaced at 16 inches, 2x6's can be used because they can span 9 feet 5 inches, which is greater than the required 8 foot spacing between the beams.

Decking Design—As shown in Table 15, 5/4 radius edge decking (RED) of redwood can be used to span the 16 inches between the joists.

Obviously, there is flexibility in choosing the spacing, size, and species for the posts, beams, joists, and decking. The deck designer is faced with trade-offs regarding the most economical and practical combination of structural member sizes. The optimal combination of member size and spacing depends on the specific requirements of your deck, available lumber species, and sizes as well as material cost.

Finally, while the members sized from these span tables will carry the loads assumed, the deck designer should keep in mind that "pushing" the tables to the limit (that is, always using the maximum span allowed for a given size joist, beam, and decking) may create a deck that, to some people at least, feels "bouncy."

Fasteners

The integrity of any wood structure is largely dependent on how its components are held together. Obviously, it makes little sense to properly design the wood members

Table 15. Maximum decking spans.

Species	Nominal Decking Size	Recommended Span
Douglas-fir, Southern pine, Hem-Fir, SPF, SPF (south), Ponderosa pine, Redwood, Western cedar	RED[a]	16"[c]
	2x4[b]	24"
	2x6[b]	24"

[a] RED is radius edge decking: 4 to 6 inch widths.
[b] Grade is No. 2 or Better.
[c] Southern pine RED can span 24 inches.

of a deck only to improperly fasten them together. This section will describe the fasteners and hardware applicable for connecting the lumber and decking used in wood deck construction and will provide recommendations regarding the types and sizes of fasteners for long-term performance.

The most common wood fasteners are nails, screws, lag screws, and bolts. Metal straps and hangers of various types are also available. Wood fasteners are typically manufactured from mild steel, though many types and sizes can be found that are made from stainless steel. Nails and screws are the most common type of fasteners used for attaching decking to the joists; for fastening the heavier structural members, such as the beams to the posts, lag screws or bolts are the fasteners of choice.

Holding-power and corrosion protection are probably the two most important concerns when choosing fasteners. Improperly specified fasteners can loosen when wood shrinks and swells as a result of moisture cycling of the exposed wood. Not only does corrosion of steel fasteners weaken the fastener, the chemical reactions involved can also weaken the surrounding wood.

Because decks are built in many different climates and exposure conditions, local conditions should dictate the proper selection of fasteners. The average outdoor humidity around the United States varies depending on location and season. In areas of higher average humidity and warmer temperatures (such as the southeastern United States) and localities exposed to salt spray, the hazard of fastener corrosion (and attack by wood-decay fungi) is greatest. Of course, even in dry areas, the moisture content of the wood in a deck can remain high, promoting corrosion, if the deck is wetted much of the time or is located above water.

Coated Fasteners

Most steel fasteners are not coated because they are intended to be used in protected environments (indoors). Obviously, if these fasteners are exposed to the weather and are not properly protected with some type of coating, they will corrode. In the mildest of cases, this corrosion can lead to unsightly staining of the wood. In more severe cases, corrosion can cause complete disintegration of the fastener and total loss of structural strength.

Several types of coatings are used to protect steel fasteners. These include paint, plastic, ceramic, and metal coatings. As the following discussion indicates, there can be considerable difference in the long-term corrosion resistance of various types of coated fasteners and their corrosion-proof counterparts.

Galvanizing is a commonly used metal coating for fasteners used in exterior environments. There is, however, considerable difference in the types of galvanized fasteners. The galvanizing (zinc, cadmium, or zinc-cadmium coating on the steel) can be applied by electroplating, mechanical plating, chemical treating, or dipping the fastener in molten zinc (hot-dipping).

Special concerns arise when fastening preservative-treated lumber below ground using CCA or ACZA treating chemicals. Waterborne preservatives that contain copper can cause accelerated corrosion of some metals. The copper salts in preservative-treated wood act as a copper cathode surrounding the fastener, while the fastener (and its metallic coating) acts as a sacrificial anode. The resulting electrolytic action slowly corrodes the fastener coating (and eventually the fastener). Obviously, the thicker the coating, the longer the protection for the fastener.

For coated fasteners, long-term exposure tests have shown that hot-dipped galvanized fasteners provide the best corrosion protection for wood that is used in damp conditions.[2] Of course, even hot-dipped galvanized fasteners will not provide adequate performance if the thickness of the zinc coating is not sufficient. Many manufacturers coat fasteners to the standard ASTM A153[3], which specifies a minimum coverage of 0.85 oz/ft^2 of zinc. This coating is probably thick enough for most decks in dryer weather areas. A thicker coating (>1.0 oz/ft^2) is available from some manufacturers and should be used in more corrosive situations.

Stainless-Steel and Aluminum Fasteners

Although more expensive than hot-dipped galvanized fasteners, stainless steel is a far better option, particularly for decks that are subject to marine exposure, are in high humidity areas, and/or remain wet much of the time. Research has shown that little long-term degradation of stainless-steel fasteners occurs, even in the severest exposure conditions.[4] Stainless-steel fasteners are available in four common grades (302, 303, 304, and 316). The higher the number, the higher the corrosion resistance (and usually the price). Grade 304 or higher is adequate for use on above-ground deck construction. The higher price of stainless-steel fasteners and hardware is often justified because the cost of the fasteners is small compared to the cost of the completed deck

---

[2] Baker, A.J. 1974. *Degradation of wood by products of metal corrosion.* Res. Pap. 229. U.S. Department of Agriculture, Forest Service, Forest Products Laboratory. Madison, WI.

[3] ASTM. 1987. *Standard specification for zinc coating (hot dip) on iron and steel hardware.* A 153-87. Philadelphia, PA: American Society for Testing and Materials. Vol. 15.08.

[4] Baker A.J. 1992. *Corrosion of nails in CCA- and ACA-treated wood in two environments.* Forest Products Journal. 42(9): 39-41.

and the fasteners add significantly to the reliability and long-term performance of the deck.

Aluminum fasteners are also available in the marketplace. However, research has shown that they rapidly corrode when in contact with all treated lumber. **Aluminum fasteners should not be used in treated wood decks.**

Recommended Fasteners and Hardware

For naturally decay-resistant species or preservative-treated wood used above ground in structures exposed to weather, it is recommended that **hot-dipped** galvanized steel fasteners be used with at least 0.85 ounce of zinc per square foot. This recommendation also applies to hardware used in the structure (joist hangers, straps). For wood that is below ground or wood in contact with salt water or spray, the use of 304 grade stainless-steel fasteners is recommended. The following text provides information on specific types of fasteners and hardware: nails, screws, lag screws and bolts, and joist hangers and metal straps.

Nails—Smooth-shanked nails often lose their holding power, when exposed to wetting and drying cycles, which can result in nail pop-up and loosening of decking boards. Although such nails are appropriate for almost all aspects of indoor house construction, deformed shank nails are recommended for construction of the deck surface. Two commonly available deformed shank nails with the capacity to retain withdrawal resistance in outdoor use are spirally grooved and annular grooved (ring-shanked) nails.

Screws—While common wood screws have been used to fasten wood for decades, the more recently developed multipurpose screw has found wide use in deck construction. Patterned after screws used to fasten gypsum wallboard, multipurpose screws (also called drywall or buglehead screws) have become very popular for securing decking boards to the joists (Fig. 21). These fasteners have a thread design for fast driving and good holding power, and unlike common wood screws, they are

Guidelines for Fastener Use

1. Use hot-dipped galvanized fasteners and hardware for deck construction.
2. Use stainless steel in very wet or highly corrosive areas (salt water or deicing salt exposure).
3. Reduce splitting of boards when nailing by
   a. Placing nails no closer to the edge than one-half of the board thickness.
   b. Predrilling nail holes (three-quarters of nail diameter). See Table 16 for sizes.
   c. Blunting the nail point.
   d. Increasing the spacing between nails.
   e. Staggering nails in each row to prevent splitting along the grain.
4. Avoid end-grain nailing where possible, because nail-holding capacity is poor.
5. Use a fastener spacing recommended by the decking board manufacturer. Two fasteners per decking board at each joist is recommended.
6. When drilling holes for lag screws or bolts, saturate the hole with preservative.
7. Use washers with bolts and lag screws to reduce wood crushing.
8. Retighten bolts and lag screws 1 year after deck construction and check tightness periodically (every 2 years).

straight shanked. Commonly available in 2- to 3-inch lengths, they are available with a phillips head or square recessed head, and are most easily driven with a power drill. Note that multipurpose screws intended for

Table 16. Nail dimensions and sizes for common nails.

Nail size	Length (in.)	Diameter (in.)
6d	2	0.113
8d	2–1/2	0.131
10d	3	0.148
12d	3–1/4	0.148
16d	3–1/2	0.162
20d	4	0.192
30d	4–1/2	0.207
40d	5	0.225
60d	6	0.263

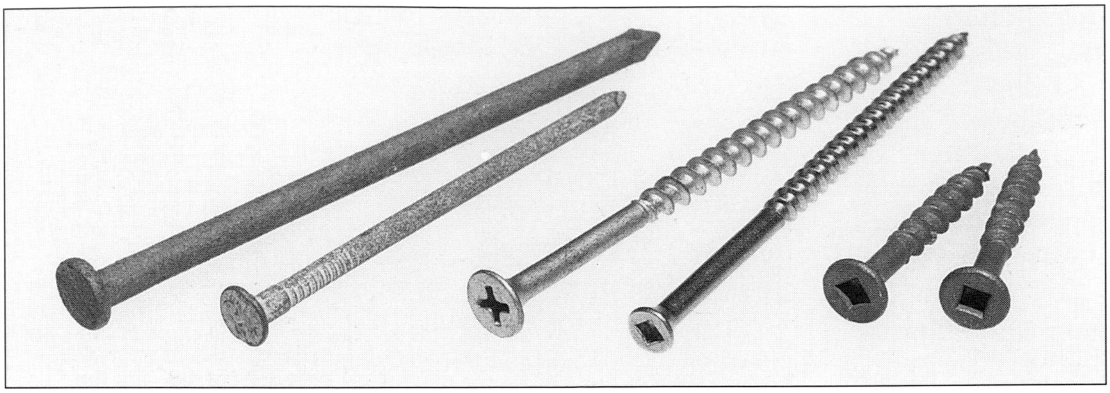

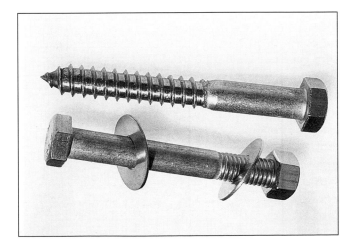

Figure 21. Galvanized nails and stainless-steel screws with different types of heads (square recess and phillips).

interior use have a black oxide coating. For wood decks, use only hot-dipped galvanized or stainless steel screws. Limit their use to fastening decking.

This type of screw is **not** intended for fastening joist hangers to beams and will not equal the design capacity of the hanger. Use only manufacturer-specified hanger nails (properly coated) to attach hangers.

Screws have an advantage over nails in that they are more easily withdrawn for removing defective or damaged decking boards. They are also effective in drawing down cupped or twisted decking boards into a flat position and will resist withdrawal over time.

Lag screws and bolts—Lag screws are commonly used to fasten one member, such as a 2 by x, to a thicker member in places where a through-bolt cannot be used (Fig. 22). Lag screws are also commonly used to secure the deck framing to the band

joist or framing of the house. Pilot holes must be drilled for lag screws, and the lag must be fully driven to be effective. Pilot holes should be about three-fourths of the diameter of the screw for the threaded portion and the full diameter for the unthreaded shank. Make sure the lag screw is long enough so that **at least half** of its length penetrates the member to which it is attached. Use a standard sized washer under the lag-screw head to reduce crushing of the wood. The washer should be sized so that its hole diameter is at most 1/8-inch larger than the bolt or lag-screw shank it is to be used with.

Bolts offer more rigidity and typically more load-carrying capacity than lag screws. However, their use is obviously limited to situations where a hole can be drilled completely through the members to be connected. Holes drilled for bolts should be no more than 1/16-inch larger in diam-

Figure 22. Fasteners for support structure. Lag screw and machine bolt shown are made of stainless steel.

eter than the size of the bolt used. Unless stated otherwise, the bolts referred to in this manual are assumed to be 1/2 inch in diameter. Use washers under both the head of the bolt and under the nut to limit crushing of the wood. Carriage bolts are not the best choice because they are designed for use without washers. After drilling holes for lag screws or bolts, saturating the holes with a preservative is recommended. For wood decks, use galvanized (hot-dipped) or stainless steel lag screws and bolts.

Joist hangers and metal straps— Joist hangers and other metal straps are often used in deck construction; however, most of these fasteners are intended for indoor use. Although typically electroplated with galvanizing, the long-term corrosion resistance of joist hangers in exposed environments is unknown. Some manufacturers do supply these products with heavier galvanized coatings for exterior use or from stainless steel, and their use is recommended for deck structures.

Construction

This section provides information on grading and drainage, footings and foundations, structural member connections, attachment of deck to the house, bracing, railing, and overhangs.

Landscaping and Drainage

A major consideration when preparing a site for deck construction is water drainage. A deck is frequently constructed over areas that were previously covered with plants or grass. Depending on the size and height of the deck, lack of light often kills these plants and bares the soil to erosion. For moderate levels of rainfall, the soils under a deck may soak up accumulated water. However, landscaping should be such that water runs away from the house. If this is not possible, some type of water collection system should be designed to carry water away from the site and prevent soil erosion. If the deck serves as a roof for a garage, carport, or living area, drainage should be treated as part of the house roof drainage and include gutters and drainpipes.

In cases where weeds can grow under a low deck, effort should be made to eliminate them. Without some control or deterrent, this growth can promote high local humidity (and high moisture contents in the wood members), resulting in increased decay hazard and accelerated fastener corrosion. This is especially true where decks are near the ground. Placing a 2- or 3-inch-thick layer of gravel under the deck (after the posts are installed) will help minimize erosion. A plastic or fabric weed barrier can also be used to help control weed growth.

Footings and Foundations

Footings or foundations are required to transfer the loads of the deck to the ground as well as to provide stability to the structure. The necessary size and depth of a footing depends on the vertical and lateral loads that the footing must carry as well as the load-bearing capacity of the soil. The correct size of concrete footings for local conditions should be available from your local building code department.

In northern areas, the depth of frost penetration also must be considered. Most building codes require that the footing be deeper than the local frost penetration to prevent frost heave. In some parts of the country, frost can penetrate 5 feet or more, requiring footings of substantial depth.

Many types of footings or foundation systems are possible. The following text describes a few choices. The details presented here differ depending on whether posts are made from preservative-treated wood (for posts in ground contact) or from a naturally decay-resistant species (for posts that do not come in contact with soil or concrete).

Figure 23 shows the simplest footings for areas with no frost hazard. These footings are usable with posts made from naturally decay-resistant or preservative-treated wood. Note that a metal post base is used to elevate the wood member from the concrete footing, protecting it from decay. The footing should bear on undisturbed or compacted earth. Because soil and other debris hold water and

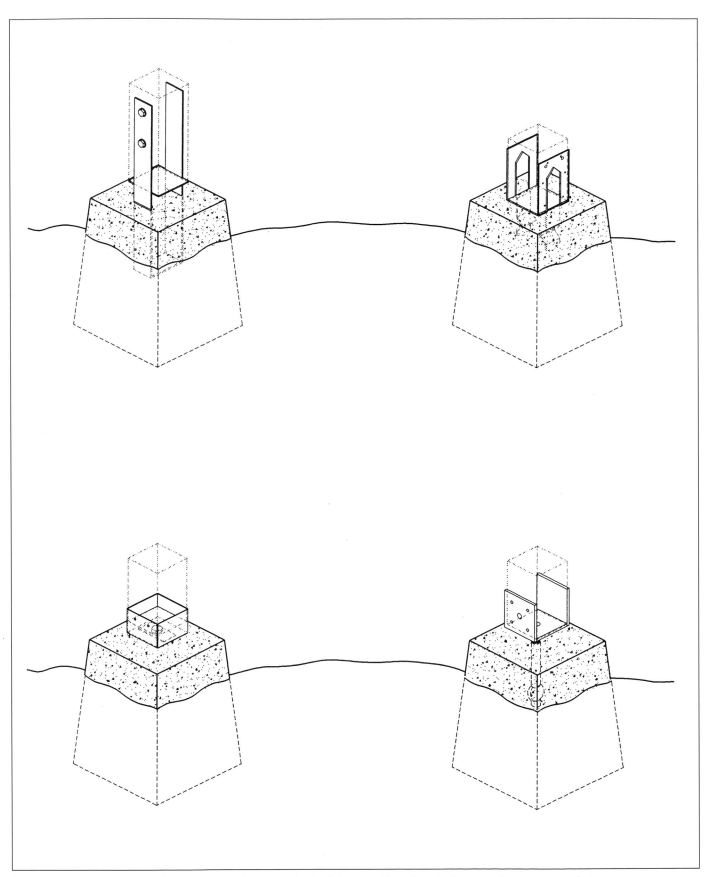

Figure 23. Footings for use in areas without ground frost. Note elevation of post above grade to prevent decay. The wood post, of a treated or a naturally decay-resistant species, should not contact the concrete.

increase the potential for decay, soil and debris should not be allowed to collect around the base of the posts. Footings can extend below the frost depth, as shown in Figure 24.

Figure 25 shows another footing for use with preservative-treated wood. Use ground contact grade posts only (0.40 lb/ft^3 retention). Note that enough concrete is used to provide a footing pad at the bottom of the hole. Set the post while the concrete is wet and wiggle the post so that it is seated in the concrete. Place at least 6 inches of concrete below the post. Note that the nails in the post are partially embedded to prevent the post from rising from the concrete. Compact the fill material around the post as the hole is refilled. Note that the cut end of the post should be field treated with a preservative.

Figure 26 shows footing connections that are decay prone and that provide little or no uplift capacity. Figure 27 illustrates what **not** to do. All the conditions shown in Figure 27 will lead to poor footing performance.

Layout of Structural Members

Because fasteners are subject to corrosion in exposed conditions, it is prudent to minimize their use where possible. The structure of the deck in Figure 28 depends entirely on the reliability of the steel fasteners and hardware to transfer deck loads. The beam is hung from the post with bolts, and the joists in turn hang from the beam with hangers. Figure 29, on the other hand, shows the joists bearing directly on the beam, which bears directly on the posts. This stacked configuration is inherently more reliable than the construction shown in Figure 28 because it does not depend entirely on load transfer through the fasteners.

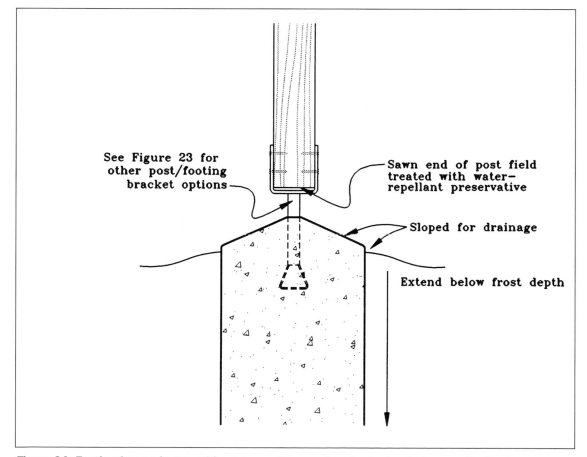

Figure 24. Footing for use in ground-frost areas. The wood post, of a treated or a naturally decay-resistant species, should not contact the concrete.

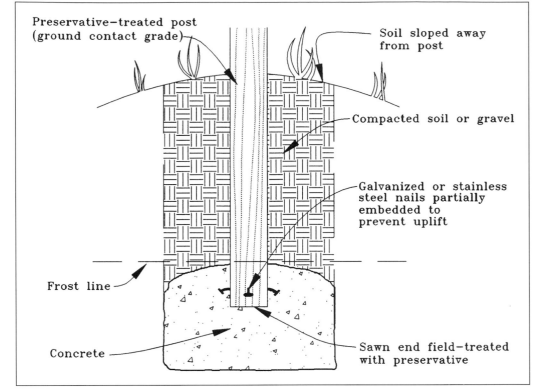

Figure 25. Simplest footing for use with preservative-treated wood.

Preservative-treated post (ground contact grade)

Soil sloped away from post

Compacted soil or gravel

Galvanized or stainless steel nails partially embedded to prevent uplift

Frost line

Concrete

Sawn end field-treated with preservative

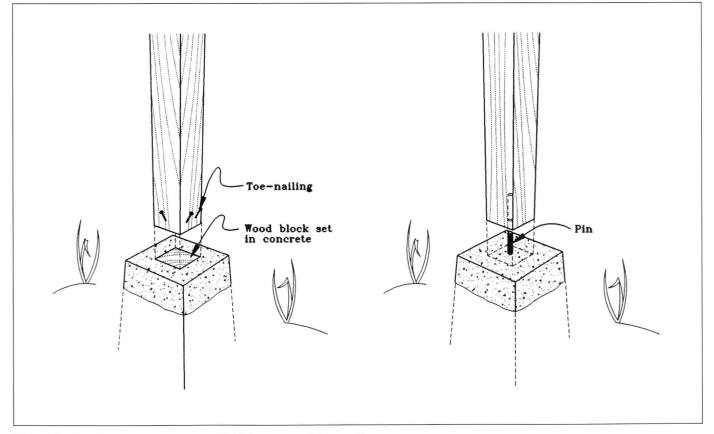

Toe-nailing

Wood block set in concrete

Pin

Figure 26. Footings prone to decay, with little or no uplift capacity.

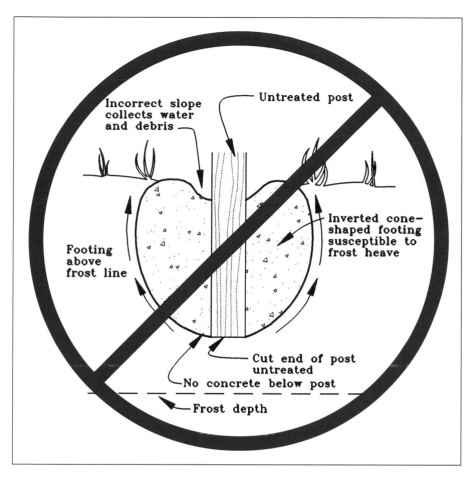

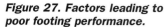

Figure 27. Factors leading to poor footing performance.

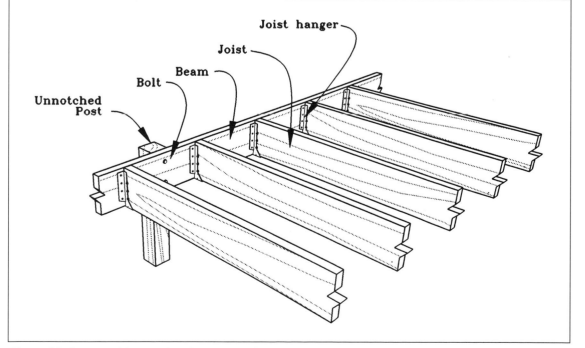

Figure 28. Structural layout that depends entirely on fasteners.

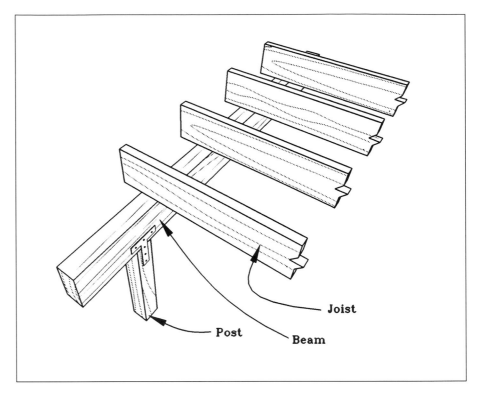

Figure 29. Structural layout that is not totally dependent on fasteners.

Joist

Post

Beam

Beam-to-post connection—The beam can be connected to the posts in several ways (Fig. 30). Note that in all these examples, the beam fully bears on the post in the connections. A galvanized or stainless steel strap, bracket, T-tie, or treated wood cleat can be used to provide stability to the connection as well as uplift resistance. Note that some of these connections adapt to both solid-sawn and built-up beams. A 1/2-inch wood spacer (preservative-treated) can be used between the members to increase the beam width to that of the supporting post (Fig. 30).

Two single 2 by x members can also be used as a beam if the post is notched to accept the single members (Fig. 31). Two bolts, a minimum of 3/8 inch in diameter, are used to tie the connection together. This notched connection is only practical for a 6x6 or larger post. Be sure to field-treat the notches with preservative before assembly.

A less desirable, but often-used, beam-to-post connection is shown in Figure 32. Although this connection is convenient to construct, its structural performance is limited by the capacity of the bolts. Based upon accepted engineering practice, there are limitations to the maximum number and size of bolts permissible for use with various 2 by x side members (Table 17). Because this connection is limited by bolt capacity, there is a maximum tributary load area that can be safely carried by each beam-to-post connection. Tables 18 and 19 show these maximum load areas for 4x4 and 6x6 posts using 1/2-inch bolts and 6x6 posts using 5/8-inch bolts, respectively. As these tables indicate, there are rather severe limitations on the loaded deck area that can be carried by a single beam-to-post connection of this type. For example, for 40-lb/ft^2 loading, assuming the use of Douglas

Table 17. Maximum number of bolts for attaching 2 by x side members to posts.

Side member size	Bolt size (diameter)	
	1/2 in.	5/8 in.
2x6	2	N/A
2x8	2	2
2x10	3	2
2x12	3	3

Fir or Southern Pine lumber, only 30 ft² of deck can be supported using a two-bolt connection. Because an interior post typically carries an area equal to the beam span times the joist span, it is obvious that this type of connection dramatically limits both the allowable beam and joist spans, requiring more posts to support the deck.

Joist-to-beam connection—The joists can be connected to the beams in a number of different ways (Fig. 33). The best configuration allows the joist to bear directly on the beam, eliminating the dependency on fastener performance. Blocking should be used to stabilize the joist. Galvanized or stainless-steel strapping can be used for

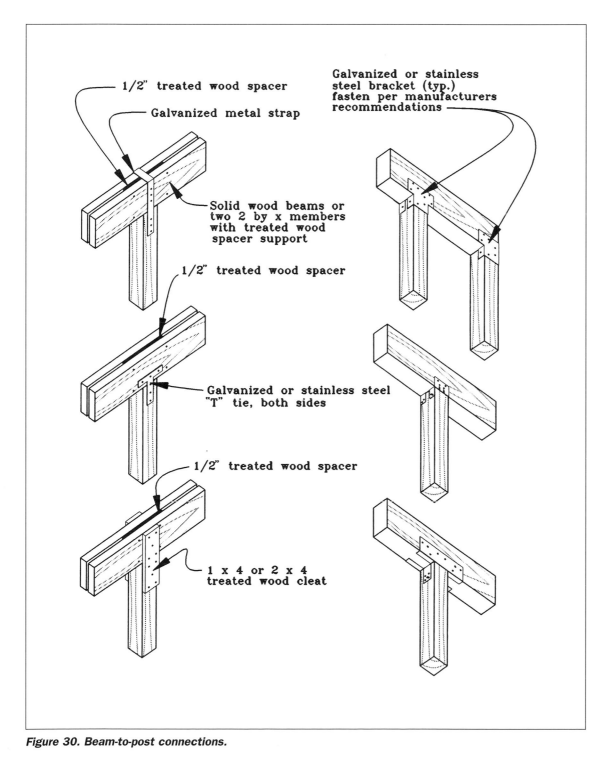

Figure 30. Beam-to-post connections.

greater uplift resistance where uplift might be a problem (or if building codes require).

Figure 34 shows often-used construction details using a 2x2 ledger to support the joists. The use of this type of connection is **not** recommended because not enough nails can be driven into the 2x2 to support the joist loads. Increasing the size of the ledger does not help, because this increases the size of the notch in the joist, reducing its load capacity. It is much better to support the joist on top of a ledger or use a joist hanger to avoid notching the joist.

Although minimizing the use of metal hardware for load transfer is suggested, joist hangers do offer lateral support to the joist and have advantages during construction.

Use only hangers and fasteners recommended by the hanger manufacturer for outdoor use (hot-dipped galvanized or stainless steel).

Decking-to-joist connection—The next member connection in a wood deck to consider is the connection of the actual decking boards to the joists. Ring-shanked nails, spirally grooved nails, or multipurpose screws are most often used and will help to prevent fastener pop-up. Only hot-dipped galvanized or stainless-steel nails or screws are recommended. As shown in Figure 35, fasten the decking according to manufacturers' recommendations **or** use two fasteners for every connection.

Table 18. Limitations in tributary load area for beam-to-post connections using 4x4 or 6x6 posts and 1/2-inch-diameter bolts.

Live load (lb/ft²)	Tributary load area (ft²)		
	Douglas–fir, Southern pine	Hem–Fir, SPF, SPF (south)	Ponderosa pine, Redwood, Western cedar
Two–bolt connection (2x6, 2x8)			
40	30	26	23
60	20	19	16
Three–bolt connection (2x10, 2x12)			
40	44	39	34
60	32	28	24

See Figure 30 for type of beam-to-post connection.

Table 19. Limitations in tributary load area for beam-to-post connections using 6x6 posts and 5/8-inch-diameter bolts.

Live load (lb/ft²)	Tributary load area (ft²)		
	Douglas–fir, Southern pine	Hem–Fir, SPF, SPF (south)	Ponderosa pine, Redwood, Western cedar
Two–bolt connection (2x8, 2x10)			
40	42	34	27
60	30	24	19
Three–bolt connection (2x12)			
40	63	51	40
60	45	37	29

See Figure 31 for type of beam-to-post connection.

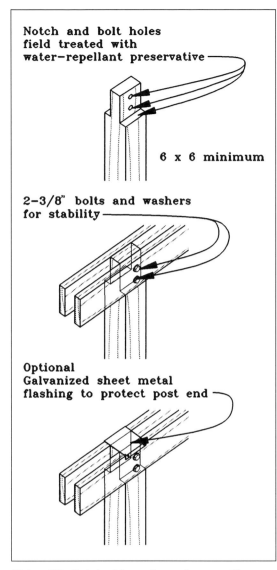

Notch and bolt holes field treated with water—repellant preservative

6 x 6 minimum

2-3/8" bolts and washers for stability

Optional Galvanized sheet metal flashing to protect post end

Figure 31. Notched beam-to-post connections using 2 by x members as beams.

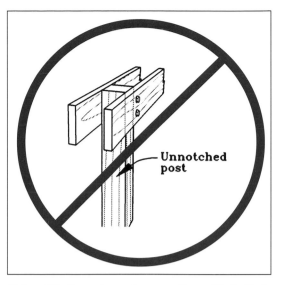

Unnotched post

Figure 32. Beam-to-post connection with limited load capacity. Not recommended.

Figure 36 shows another option for connecting the decking to the joists. The double joist serves to fasten the ends of the decking boards more substantially to the joists and to provide an airspace between the butt ends of the decking boards (prevents collection of moisture and debris at the ends and reduces the potential for decay). Obviously, using this double-joist detail requires extra joists.

Several products are available for fastening decking boards that eliminate the use of nails or screws on the decking boards surface. While these products provide a smooth appearance to the deck surface, they may make it more difficult to repair or replace individual decking boards if the need arises (Fig. 37).

Attachment of Deck to House

Where practical, the best construction technique is to build the deck so that it is freestanding, as shown in Figure 38. Although an extra row of posts and beams is needed in a freestanding deck, this practice eliminates the penetration of the weatherproof siding of the house.

If properly done, it is possible to attach a deck to the house using a 2 by x without opening the protective envelope of the siding to the entry of moisture, which can lead to decay problems (see Fig. 39). Investigations of deck collapses show that most failures were caused by decay, improper fastening of the deck to the house, or the inability of the structural framing of the house to carry the deck loads. In at least one case, even though the deck was firmly attached to the band joist of the house, the connection between the band joist and house floor joist failed when the deck was under load. This example indicates the importance of assuring that the deck is adequately attached to the house and that the framing in the house is adequate to handle the deck loads.

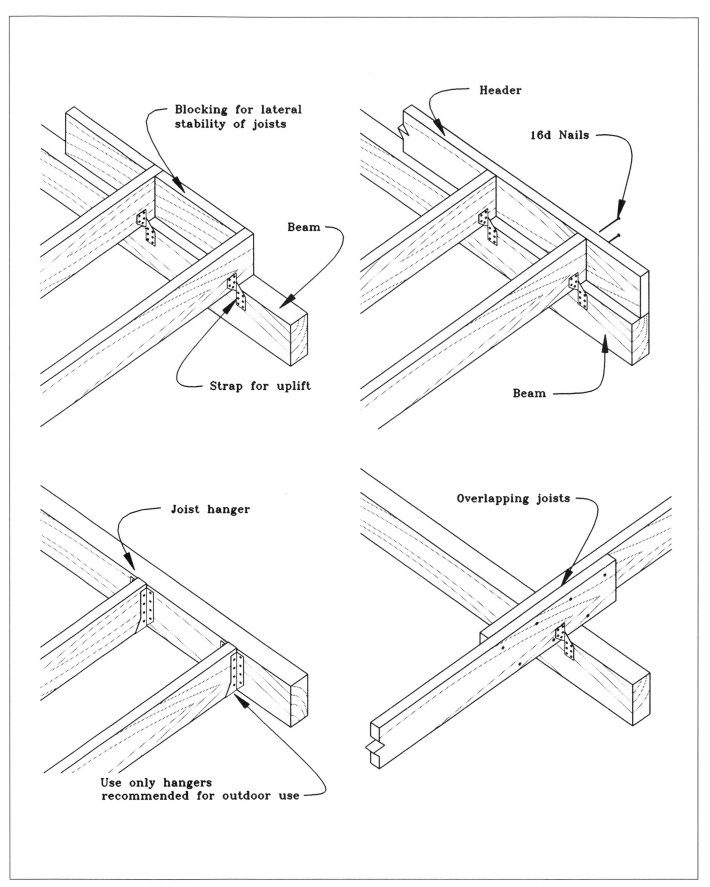

Figure 33. Joist-to-beam connections.

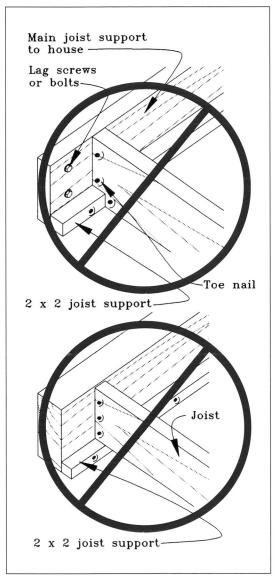

Main joist support to house

Lag screws or bolts

Toe nail

2 x 2 joist support

Joist

2 x 2 joist support

Figure 34. 2x2 joist supports. Not recommended.

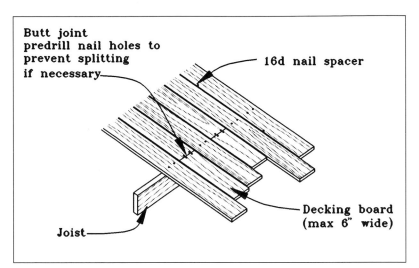

Butt joint predrill nail holes to prevent splitting if necessary

16d nail spacer

Joist

Decking board (max 6" wide)

Figure 35. Decking board nailing.

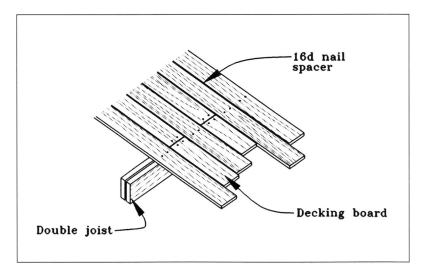

16d nail spacer

Double joist

Decking board

Figure 36. Use of double joist for attachment of deck boards.

Figure 37. Products for concealed fastening of decking boards.

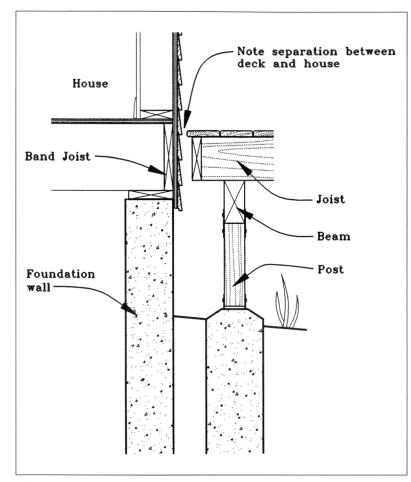

House

Note separation between deck and house

Band Joist

Foundation wall

Joist

Beam

Post

Figure 38. Freestanding deck.

For the design shown in Figure 39, it is essential to provide proper weatherproofing (using metal flashing) in attaching the deck to the house. Carefully caulk the bolt holes to assure that water does not enter the main structure of the house. Washer spacers assure drying of the 2 by x attaching the deck to the house and protection from decay.

Figure 39 shows one option for attaching the deck to the house. The lag screws or bolts should fasten to the band joist, plate, or wall studs. Occasionally, this may require additional blocking or additional reinforcement of the framing of the house. Using only nails to secure the deck to the house is **not** adequate. Note that bolts are used (where possible) for higher structural-load capacity.

If the 2 by x is attached to the band joist, the deck designer must make sure the band joist is firmly attached to the house framing and can resist the tendency for the deck to pull away from the house. For new house construction, the nailing shown in Figure 40, A is recommended for all zones of the house (particularly second stories) that might have a deck or porch attached at a future date. For existing construction, access to the top and bottom of the band joist is often impossible when attaching a deck. Toenailing into the sole and sill plates above and below the 2 by x (after removing the siding) as shown in Figure 40, B will secure the band joist.

Table 20 shows the number of lag screws or bolts needed to attach the deck to the house as a function of the joist span and spacing (assuming the joists are perpendicular to the house). Remember that lag screws will be effective only if they penetrate the band joist of the house or the wall studs at least 1-1/2 inches and if the band joist is securely attached to the structural framing of the house.

Bracing

Decks that are not held in place laterally through rigid attachment to the house need bracing to assure that they remain structurally stable.

In a wood-frame house, the sheathing or let-in bracing serves to stabilize the walls against lateral instability. Because a deck does not use sheathing, bracing is needed to provide resistance to lateral instability. This is especially critical for elevated decks or those constructed on uneven or sloping lots, which may require long posts.

Where practical, the angle bracing shown in Figure 41 should be used at the post-to-beam connection. For the sides of a deck where angle bracing is impractical, longer braces can be used (Figs. 17 and 42). When the unsupported length of the brace is less than about 8 feet, 2x4 braces can be used. For greater unsupported lengths, 2x6 bracing is recommended. A minimum of 3/8-inch bolts should be used to connect the bracing to the main members of the deck.

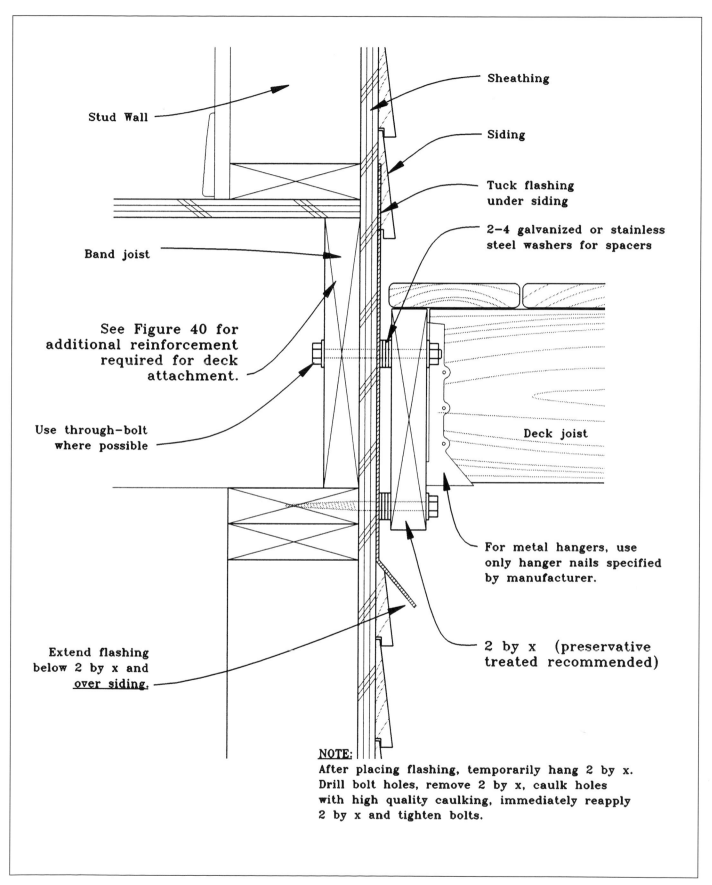

Stud Wall

Sheathing

Siding

Tuck flashing
under siding

Band joist

2-4 galvanized or stainless
steel washers for spacers

See Figure 40 for
additional reinforcement
required for deck
attachment.

Deck joist

Use through-bolt
where possible

For metal hangers, use
only hanger nails specified
by manufacturer.

Extend flashing
below 2 by x and
<u>over siding.</u>

2 by x (preservative
treated recommended)

<u>NOTE:</u>
After placing flashing, temporarily hang 2 by x.
Drill bolt holes, remove 2 by x, caulk holes
with high quality caulking, immediately reapply
2 by x and tighten bolts.

Figure 39. Deck attachment to house.

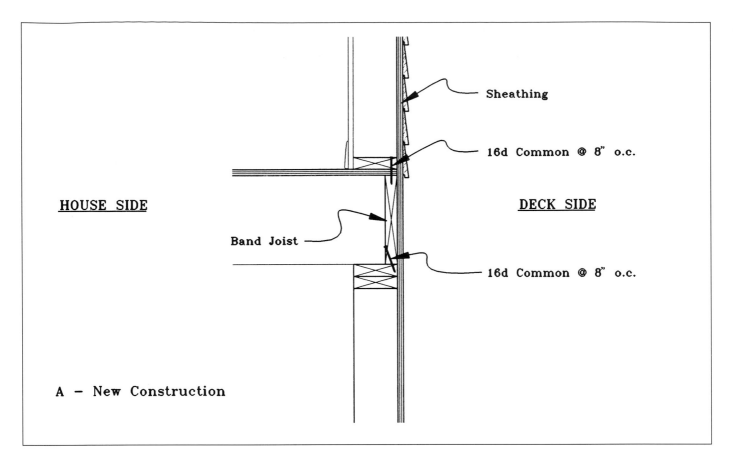

HOUSE SIDE

DECK SIDE

Sheathing

16d Common @ 8" o.c.

Band Joist

16d Common @ 8" o.c.

A — New Construction

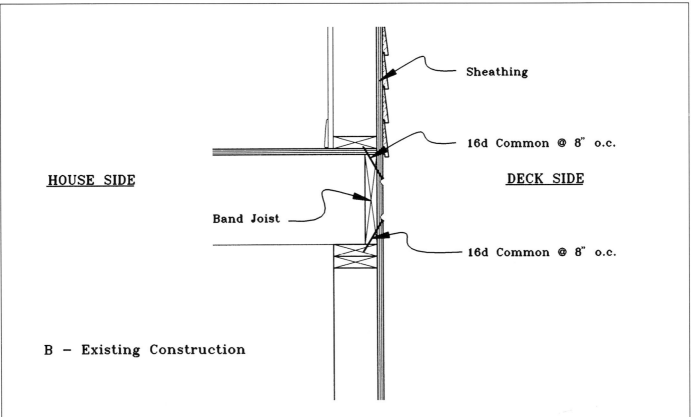

HOUSE SIDE

DECK SIDE

Sheathing

16d Common @ 8" o.c.

Band Joist

16d Common @ 8" o.c.

B — Existing Construction

Figure 40. Suggested nailing at probable deck locations to strengthen band joist-to-deck connection.

Table 20. Recommended number, diameter, and spacing of lag screws or bolts for attaching deck to house for a given joist span and spacing using a 2 by x of the same depth as the deck joists. Limitations of Table 17 apply.

Joist spacing		Joist span		
		0–6 ft	6–12 ft	12–16 ft
40 lb/ft²	12 in.	(2) – 3/8 in. @ 24 in.	(2) – 1/2 in. @ 24 in.	(2) – 1/2 in. @ 24 in.
	16 in.	(2) – 3/8 in. @ 24 in.	(2) – 1/2 in. @ 24 in.	(2) – 1/2 in. @ 24 in.
	24 in.	(2) – 3/8 in. @ 24 in.	(2) – 1/2 in. @ 24 in.	(2) – 1/2 in. @ 24 in.
60 lb/ft²	12 in.	(2) – 3/8 in. @ 24 in.	(2) – 1/2 in. @ 24 in.	(2) – 1/2 in. @ 18 in.
	16 in.	(2) – 3/8 in. @ 16 in.	(2) – 1/2 in. @ 16 in.	(2) – 1/2 in. @ 16 in.
	24 in.	(2) – 1/2 in. @ 24 in.	(2) – 5/8 in. @ 24 in.	(2) – 5/8 in. @ 20 in.

Number of lag screws or bolts given in parentheses.

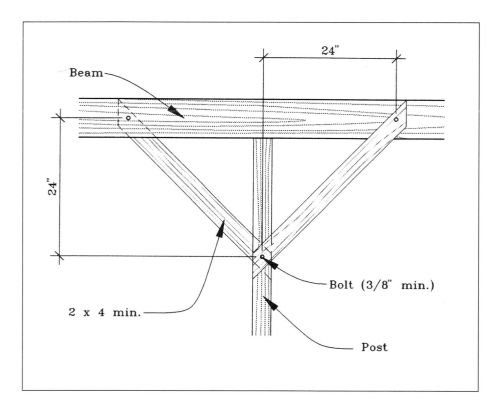

Figure 41. Post-to-beam bracing.

The simplest bracing systems using single members are shown in Figure 42, A and B. Another system of bracing used between posts is the X or cross brace (Fig. 42, C). For long beam spans or high posts, a cross brace can be used at every bay. Normally, however, bracing at alternate bays is sufficient. Where posts are 14 feet or more high, which can occur on very steep slopes, two braces per bay might be required to avoid the use of an excessively long brace or K brace (Fig. 42, D). When fastening braces, care should be taken so moisture cannot be trapped and end grain is not directly exposed to rain. Figure 43 shows suggested and **not** recommended bracing connections.

Railings

For obvious safety reasons, most building codes require a railing for any deck that is more than a given distance off the ground (often 18 to 24 inches). The railing (often 42 inches high) must include intermittent balusters placed such that a sphere (usually

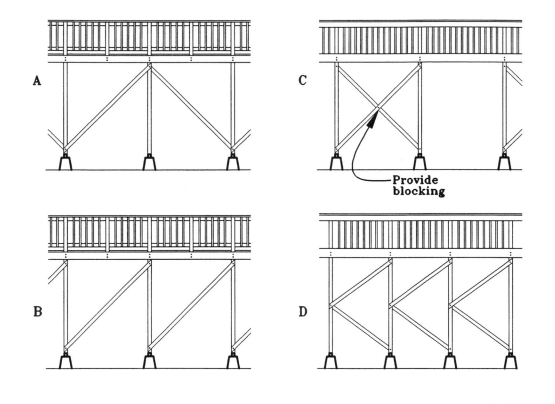

Figure 42. Types of post-to-post braces.

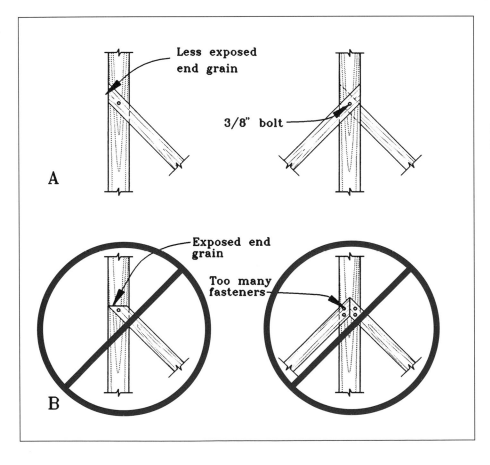

Figure 43. Bracing connections: (A) suggested; (B) not recommended.

4-inch diameter) cannot pass through. The railing must resist the lateral loads of people leaning on or running into it.

The perimeter support posts can be incorporated in the railing of the deck. As shown in Figure 44, the posts extend from the footing to the top of the railing cap. Balusters are used to fill between the railing posts. The advantage of this design is that the full length of the post resists the rail load. Note that 6x6 posts are suggested in this situation if the beams are to be notched into the posts.

Main railing posts should be spaced at a maximum of about 6 feet apart. Balusters can be used between these posts in combination with cap rail and bottom rail to transfer the rail loads to the posts.

Figure 45, A shows an alternative for securing an attached rail post. The post should be firmly bolted to either the joist or beam, depending on the construction configuration. Avoid the type of notched railing post shown in Figure 45, B because the post is prone to splitting.

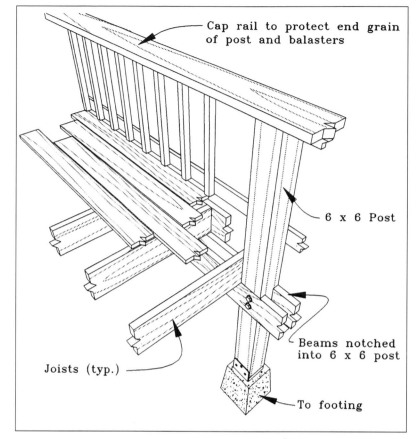

Figure 44. Deck-to-railing connection using perimeter posts.

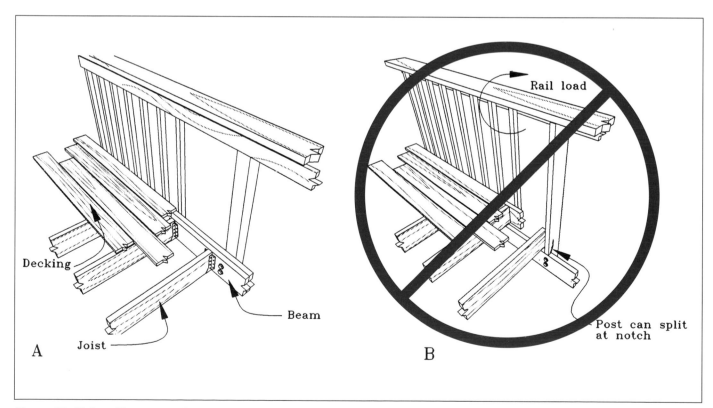

Figure 45. Main railing connections: (A) acceptable; (B) connection prone to splitting.

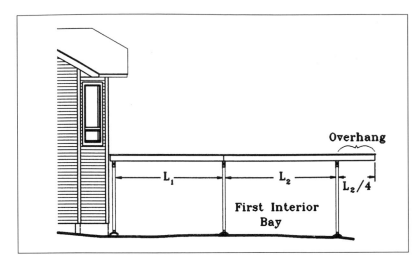

Figure 46. Limitations on overhang length.

Overhangs

It is often desirable to overhang a deck for aesthetics or for extending the deck beyond solid footing areas. Certain considerations must be taken into account when using an overhang. The length of the overhang should be limited to 25 percent of the joist span of the first interior bay (Fig. 46).

A concentrated load on the overhang has the effect of producing uplift on the joist at the first interior post support (or at the house attachment), as shown in Figure 47. Where such an uplift is anticipated, a steel twist strap will effectively transfer the uplift force into the beam, through the post, and into the footing, assuming all these members are properly connected (Fig. 47). Note that a full-length joist must be used to span from the interior post (A in Fig. 47) to the end of the overhang.

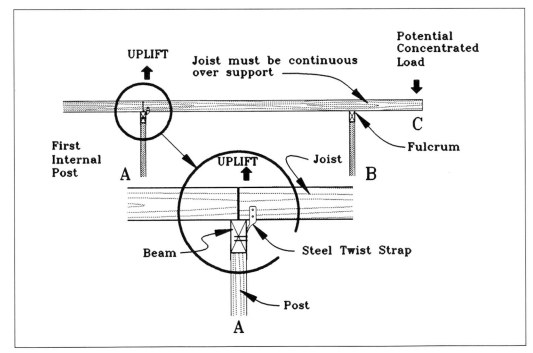

Figure 47. Effect of concentrated load on overhang: uplift produced at first interior support.
Inset shows use of steel twist straps (at each joist) to prevent uplift.

4

▲ ▲ ▲ ▲ ▲ ▲ ▲ ▲ ▲ ▲ ▲ ▲ ▲ ▲ ▲ ▲ ▲ ▲ ▲ ▲

FINISHING OF DECKS

The performance of wood as a building material for decks depends on its properties, which include engineering properties, finishing characteristics, and maintenance requirements. Poor finish performance, mildew growth, checking and splitting, and decay can be minimized with proper finishing procedures. If the deck is properly finished initially, and maintained periodically, it will be both aesthetically pleasing and longer lasting.

The horizontal surface of the deck, foot traffic, and full exposure to sun and rain make deck finishing more demanding than other wood finishing (i.e., exterior walls and interior floors). The various types of finishes appropriate for decks, application techniques, and expected service-life on both preservative-treated and untreated lumber will be summarized in this chapter, with the primary focus on newly constructed decks.

Types of Finishes

Finishes fall into two categories: those that penetrate the wood surface (do not form a film) and those that do not penetrate

> Lumber should **not** be left unfinished for 6 months to a year as indicated in some product literature or as recommended by some paint and lumber suppliers.

the wood (do form a film). The primary function of any wood finish is to protect the surface of the wood from natural weathering processes (sunlight and water) and to help maintain its appearance.

The way in which a binder is formulated into a finish determines whether the finish forms a film on the wood surface or penetrates the wood surface leaving no distinct layer or coating. Film-forming materials include paints of all descriptions, solid-color stains, varnishes, and lacquers. Penetrating finishes include water repellants, water-repellant preservatives, semitransparent (pigmented) stains, and chemical treatments.

Figure 48. Deck treated with water-repellant preservative.

Penetrating Finishes

The advantage of a penetrating finish over one that forms a film is that the wood can breathe and the finish cannot peel. Penetrating finishes repel water, thus protecting against the damaging effects of moisture. Penetrating finishes can be used as a pretreatment for other finishes or as the finish itself.

Water repellants and water-repellant preservatives—The difference between a water repellant and a water-repellant preservative (WRP) is that the WRP includes a mildewcide which provides mildew resistance. Both finish types contain a water repellant, such as wax, and a binder, but do not contain pigments. The amount of water repellant varies among brands. Some preservatives are formulated with a low concentration of water repellant so that they can be used as a pretreatment for other finishes (about 1 percent by volume). Others are formulated with a high concentration of water repellant (about 3 percent by volume) and are meant to be used as stand-alone finishes.

Application of a water repellant or WRP enhances the performance of the treated wood deck in many ways. The water repellant decreases the amount of water absorption during rain and snow, thus decreasing the dimensional changes in the wood. Less dimensional change in the wood results in less splitting, cracking, warping, and twisting.

The WRP binder is usually 10 to 20 percent and is often a drying oil (linseed or tung oil) or a varnish. These oils or diluted varnishes penetrate the wood surface and then cure to partially seal the wood surface. They also help bind the mildewcide (fungicide) and water repellant to the wood surface. These finishes are extremely effective in stopping the absorption of liquid water (Fig. 48).

For naturally decay-resistant wood species, WRPs provide mildew resistance for both the heartwood and sapwood. If the lumber contains sapwood, treatment with a WRP provides some measure of aboveground decay resistance.

The waterborne preservative treatments used to treat lumber (i.e., chromated copper

Figure 49. Mildew growth on preservative-treated decking boards. Portion of one board was washed with bleach solution to remove mildew.

arsenate) do not contain mildewcides (Fig. 49). Mildew resistance is provided by treating preservative-treated wood with a WRP. The WRP also provides some aboveground decay resistance for sections of the wood that either did not take the preservative treatment (heartwood) or that were exposed by cutting or drilling.

Water-repellant preservatives formulated with nondrying oils that act as solvents (such as paraffin oil) are also available. These oils penetrate the wood, but do not dry. Therefore, the deck surface may remain oily until the finish is absorbed. This absorption process may take several days depending on the application rate and porosity of the wood. These products are easy to apply to decks and have the same results and durability as other WRP finishes.

Semitransparent stains—When pigments are added to WRP solutions or to similar transparent wood finishes, the mixture is classified as a semitransparent stain (Fig. 50). Semitransparent stains are suitable for both preservative-treated and naturally decay-resistant wood. Addition of pigment provides color and greatly

increases the service life of the finish. Semitransparent stains permit the wood grain to show through. Stains penetrate into the wood without forming a continuous film layer and, consequently, will not blister or peel, even if excessive moisture enters the wood. The pigment protects the wood surface from sunlight, thus increasing the service life. The binder in the solventborne oil-based semitransparent stain absorbs into the wood surface as does a WRP, so a film does not form.

The durability of a stain system depends on the amount and type of its pigment, resin, preservative, and water repellant, the wood species and its surface characteristics, and the quantity of material applied to the wood surface. Semitransparent stains, originally formulated for use on siding, are now manufactured specifically for use on decks. These formulations have improved abrasion resistance; they are usually labeled as a Deck Stain or the user instructions indicate that they are formulated for use on decks.

If the decking boards were treated with a WRP in the factory or if they were recently finished with a WRP, an applied

Southern Pine

Cedar

Figure 50. Oil-based solventborne semitransparent stain on southern pine and cedar.

semitransparent stain may not absorb properly. In these situations, the wood should be allowed to weather for 2 to 3 months before finishing. This is the **only** situation where it is beneficial to wait before finishing wood with a semitransparent stain. The rate of absorption by water can be used as a guide to determine

when to refinish wood with a penetrating finish. If water is sprinkled on the deck and it quickly absorbs, the deck is probably ready to be refinished.

Mildewcides—Mildewcides are added to finishes to stop or slow the growth of surface mold and mildew (Fig. 51), which discolor the surface. Mildewcides can be formulated in WRPs, semitransparent stains, solid-color stains, and paints and are applied to naturally decay-resistant species and to preservative-treated wood. The mildewcides used in WRPs differ from chromated copper arsenate (CCA), ammoniacal copper zinc arsenate (ACZA), and other factory-applied preservatives. Waterborne preservative treatments are effective only against decay fungi. The following mildewcides are contained in WRPs available to the consumer (except pentachlorophenol) and are formulated for brush application:

3-Iodo-2-propynyl butyl carbamate (commonly called "Polyphase"): used in several commercial clear and WRP formulations and pigmented stains. It is available in both solventborne and waterborne systems at approximately 0.5 percent composition by weight.

2-(Thiocyanomethylthio) benzothiazole (TCMTB): alone or in combination with methylene bis (thiocyanate) (MTC or MTB); may also be effective as a mildewcide for WRP and stain formulations. It is available in both solventborne and waterborne formulations and the concentrations required are 0.5 percent by weight of each component.

Zinc naphthanate: available commercially in WRP formulations and possibly in some new stains and in solventborne and waterborne formulations. Approximately 2 percent composition by weight of zinc metal is suggested.

Figure 51. Moss, mildew, and lichens on deck railing.

Copper naphthanate: available commercially in WRPs and in solventborne and waterborne formulations. Approximately 2 percent composition by weight of copper metal is recommended. This mildewcide tints the wood green and therefore is not popular for use on visible portions of decks. However, it is very effective for use on cut ends of posts before placing them in the ground. It is one of the few mildewcides that is also used in pressure treatment of wood for below-ground decay resistance.

Copper-8-quinolinolate: available in commercial WRPs and may be available in stains. Like copper naphthanate, copper-8-quinolinolate turns the wood green. Effective concentrations range from 0.25 to 0.675 percent.

Mixture of bis (tributyltin) oxide and N-trichloromethylthio phthalimide: available in several commercial stain formulations at 0.5 to 1.0 percent composition by weight. N-trichloromethylthio phthalimide is also called Folpet.

Pentachlorophenol (penta): used quite extensively in WRP formulations until about 1980, it is no longer readily available to the consumer in either the ready-to-use formulation (5 percent penta) or the concentrated (40 percent penta) formulation because of its high toxicity and status as a carcinogen. Pentachlorophenol can only be used by registered pesticide applicators.

Some European commercial WRP formulations available in the United States may contain preservatives other than those listed above.

New penetrating finishes—Before 1980, WRP formulations were primarily solventborne. Since then, several waterborne formulations have become available. In addition, several manufacturers are marketing low volatile organic compound formulations for use in some areas. Volatile organic compound (VOC) is a general term for solvents and co-solvents used in both solventborne and waterborne finishes. Almost all states have legislation in place or pending that limits the VOC levels in architectural finishes. This legislation has greatly affected the formulation of penetrating finishes, and a number of low VOC water repellant and water-repellant preservatives are available for use in these areas.

Figure 52. Poor performance from a solid-color (nonpenetrating) stain. Not recommended; very difficult to repair.

Figure 53. Deck railing painted with high performance architectural coating. (Sealing end-grain of individual ballusters with water repellant before assembly will enhance performance.)

Film-Forming Finishes

Film-forming finishes encompass a wide range of finishes—from waterborne latex-based semitransparent stains to paints, including both oil-based and latex solid-color stains (also called opaque stains).

Most of these products are **unsuitable** for use on decks.

Latex   semitransparent stains—Waterborne semitransparent latex-based stains are emulsions of polymers (usually acrylics or acrylic blends). Waterborne latex-based stains do not penetrate the wood surface because the polymers' molecular weights are too high. As a result, these polymers form thin films on the wood surface. They have the disadvantage that as films, they are subject to peeling and generally tend to check, particularly when applied to species having wide bands of dense latewood, such as southern pine. Latex semitransparent stains are **not** recommended by the manufacturer for use on decks.

Oil and latex solid-color stains—Oil and latex solid-color stains are also available, but should **not** be used on decks (Fig. 52). These products, also called heavy-bodied or opaque stains, are essentially similar to paint because of their film-forming characteristics. Such stains, which can be oil- or latex-based (solvent- or waterborne), can be used successfully on siding and panel products such as hardboard.

Paints—Paints are commonly divided into oil-based (solvent-borne) and latex-based (waterborne) systems (Fig. 53). Of the available wood finishes, paints provide the greatest protection against weathering and offer the widest selection of colors. A paint film will retard penetration of moisture and decrease problems of discoloration by wood extractives. Proper selection of pigments can essentially eliminate ultraviolet (UV) light degradation of the wood surface (see section on Weathering). However, paint is not a preservative; it will not prevent decay if conditions are favorable for fungal growth

Figure 54. Cracking and peeling of varnish on exterior wood.

(see subsection in Weathering on Wood-finish interaction).

It is **not** recommended to use paint on decks. However, if paint is your only choice because of color limitations or desire for a certain appearance, a few procedures can extend the paint's service life. The lumber should be finished initially with a WRP and the end-grain primed before construction.

If highly-colored woods such as red-wood or cedar are to be painted, they require a stain-blocking primer. Such primers are formulated to prevent the colored extractives in the wood from bleeding through the paint. They are identifiable by wording on the container, such as "specially formulated for priming exterior wood," "stops wood-dye staining," "eliminates staining," or "helps eliminate extractives bleed."

Varnishes and lacquers—Varnishes and lacquers are **not** recommended for finishing decks. Clear varnishes or lacquers do allow all the natural color and grain pattern of wood to show and give the wood an attractive initial appearance. Unfortunately, varnish finishes, when exposed to sun and rain, typically last less than a year (Fig. 54). Also, these finishes must be removed before refinishing.

The short-term performance of varnishes is caused by the lack of pigments that protect wood from UV-light degradation. The addition of colorless UV-light absorbers to clear finishes has been only moderately successful in extending the durability of these clear coatings. The weatherproof qualities of even relatively durable, clear synthetic polymers are limited because UV light penetrates the transparent film and degrades the underlying wood. As the wood at the interface degrades, the varnish loses adhesion.

Lacquers and shellacs are **not** suitable as exterior clear finishes for wood because of their sensitivity to water and embrittlement after only a few months of exposure.

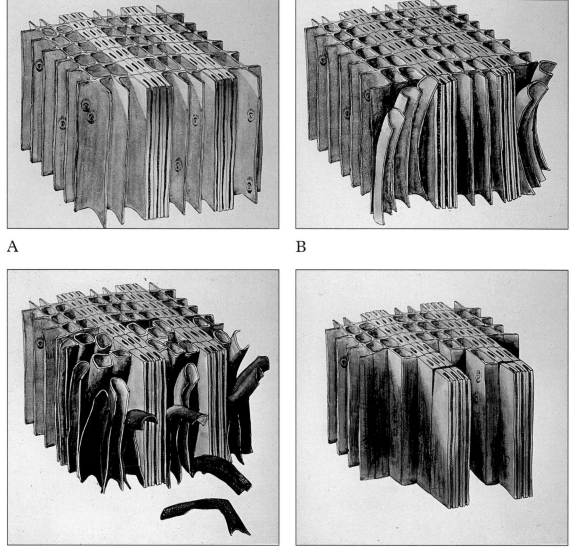

A

B

C

D

Figure 55. Schematic of wood surface erosion caused by UV radiation and water. (A) Unexposed wood; (B) early phase of weathering showing loosening of fibers; (C) early phase of fiber loss; and (D) later phase showing primarily loss of less-dense earlywood, leading to a "washboard" surface.

Factors That Affect Finishes

The performance of finishes is affected by weathering, wood species, wood quality and grade, preservative treatment, and moisture content.

Weathering

Weathering is a photochemical degradation of the wood surface caused by the combined effects of sunlight (UV radiation), water, and abrasion by wind-blown sand or other particulates. Weathering affects the wood, the finish, and the wood/finish interface. Color changes occur in wood as it weathers. Weathering is a natural process for all materials, and in wood this process can lead to a driftwood-grey weathered finish. This weathered look is often desirable for some uses (shakes, shingles, and siding), but for decks, some

Figure 56. Western cedar exposed to weather for 8 years: (A) weathered specimen with top half protected by a metal strip; (B) micrograph of weathered surface.

protection is necessary to avoid checking, cracking, and splintering.

Wood—Weathering of wood should not be confused with decay. Photochemical degradation is manifested by an initial color change, followed by loosening of wood fibers and gradual erosion of the wood surface (Fig. 55). Rain washes the degraded wood materials from the surface. Rain and/or changes in humidity cause dimensional changes in the wood that accelerate this erosion process. Erosion is more rapid in the less-dense earlywood than in the latewood, which leads to an uneven surface (Fig. 56). Over time, the wood surface erodes (Fig. 57), depending on the exposure, the species, and the intensity of UV radiation.

The color of most preservative-treated wood when it arrives at the job site is either

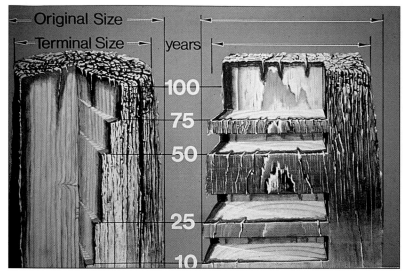

Figure 57. Artist's rendition of surface changes in post with more than 100 years of weathering. Bottom of post shows early phase of weathering (slight color change and checking). Top of post shows substantial wood loss and deep cracks.

light green (from the copper and chromium salts in the preservative) or brown (from added dye). Cedar and redwood have the freshly sawn natural color of these species. These colors will change and eventually the surface will age. The rate at which the surface will age depends on the care that the deck receives. Sunlight can begin to change the surface color of wood within days. Darker woods, such as redwood and cedar, tend to become lighter, whereas light-colored woods, such as pine, tend to become darker.

Finish—The wood finish also undergoes photochemical degradation, but the mode of degradation is different for a penetrating finish (stains and water repellants) and a film-forming finish (paints). The

weathering of penetrating finishes such as semitransparent stains and WRPs is similar to that of unfinished wood. The penetrating finish degrades, but at a slower rate than that of unfinished wood. If the finish contains a pigment (semitransparent stain), the pigment partially blocks the sunlight. As the wood surface and the finish undergo simultaneous degradation, the pigment particles debond. As the pigment erodes from the surface, the wood begins to degrade. Timely refinishing is essential to avoid excessive wood degradation.

Pigmented film-forming finishes, such as paints, block the damaging UV radiation and protect the wood surface. The degradation of the film occurs at the surface of the film and results in slow erosion of the finish. This is the most benign mode of paint degradation because as the primer coat begins to show, another topcoat can be applied. Where the paint/wood system is protected from direct exposure to the weather, a good paint system will protect the wood surface indefinitely. These uses include siding and porches where the paint is protected by a roof.

Wood-finish interaction—Finishing a wood deck presents problems that are not encountered in other exterior wood finishing applications. Decks are fully exposed to the weather (i.e., sunlight and moisture) and the wood is exposed in a horizontal position that results in the most intense exposure to sunlight and water ponding, leaving wet surfaces for extended periods. Sunlight and moisture affect different parts of the wood/finish system: the most important factor in the degradation of unfinished wood and finish surfaces is the UV portion of sunlight.

The common factor for wood decay and paint peeling is water. Moisture causes shrinking and swelling of wood, which stress film-forming finishes. Besides these stresses, water at the film/wood interface can increase the chance for peeling of the film by degrading the bond between the wood and the film.

In structures that are fully exposed to the weather, such as decks and railings, film-

A water-repellant preservative (WRP) is the easiest finish to maintain on a deck. The next best finish is a semitransparent oil-based stain. Film-forming finishes such as paint are prone to fail by peeling and are **not** recommended for decks. Although water repellants require more frequent application than other kinds of finishes, the ease of refinishing compensates for the increased frequency of application.

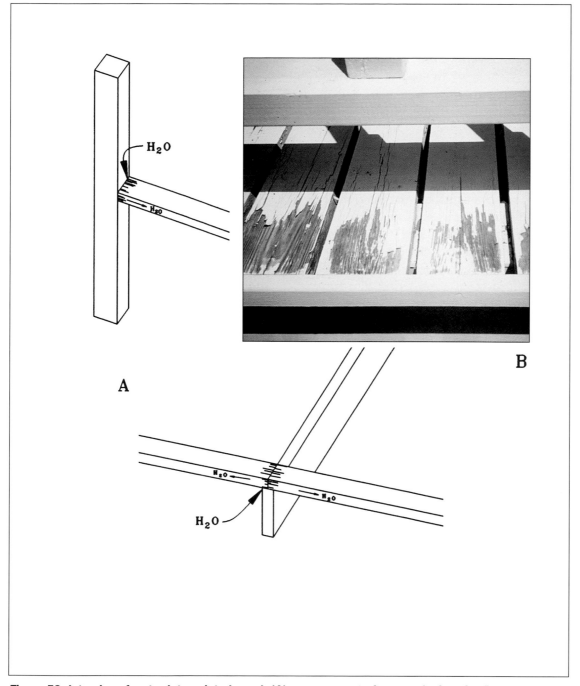

Figure 58. Intrusion of water into painted wood: (A) areas prone to form cracks in paint film; (B) paint failure caused by water intrusion.

forming finishes can trap moisture. The paint seal breaks at the joints between different pieces of wood. Water enters at these breaks and moves along the grain under the paint film (Fig. 58). This film traps the moisture; over the course of several cyclic wetting and drying conditions, the moisture content of the wood continues to increase.

This increased moisture can lead to decay conditions in the wood and weakening of the paint bond. The paint will peel at these joints.

Species

Wood species that are normally used for decks have a range of characteristics that affect the performance of the finish in different ways. These characteristics include density, weathering, percentage of latewood, dimensional stability, and decay resistance. Penetrating finishes for wood decks are not as sensitive to species as are film-forming finishes. However, more frequent applications of penetrating finishes are necessary to minimize surface checking. The lower density woods, such as redwood, accept all finishes very well. The higher density woods, such as the southern pines, typically require more frequent maintenance of all finishes as a result of the presence of wide, high-density latewood bands. Dimensional stability is better in lower density woods than higher density species, an important factor if considering film-forming finishes.

Wood Quality and Grade

Lumber grades are used to sort lumber into quality ranges; a higher lumber grade may be desirable when selecting a finish for a particular aesthetic appearance. The presence, size, and condition of knots in lumber have little effect on the performance of penetrating finishes, but these factors can cause problems with film-forming finishes. Knots do not absorb stain as readily as the surrounding wood, and their presence is often accentuated by some finishes. Knots also contain more pitch and high concentrations of wood resins. Pitch and resins can exude from the knot into the finish and cause discoloration.

Pitch bleed can occur in softwoods like pine and Douglas-fir that have not been kiln-dried. Wood with pitch bleed on its surface will not accept and hold a finish properly. The problem is often difficult to see until after the deck is constructed and the wood is heated by the sun. The remedy for avoiding pitch bleed is to purchase wood that has been kiln-dried. Pitch is set during the kiln-drying process when the high temperatures drive off the turpentine, causing the pitch to become much less fluid. Occasional pitch bleed can sometimes be removed with mineral spirits or turpentine. Little else can be done if the pitch bleed is severe, short of replacing the problem boards.

Preservative-Treated Wood

One waterborne preservative treatment, chromated copper arsenate (CCA), improves the life expectancy and durability of semitransparent stains and similar finishes. This preservative contains chromium oxides that bond to the wood after treatment. The chromium oxides decrease the photodegradation of the wood surface below the semitransparent stain and can thereby increase the durability of the stain by a factor of two or three. Other waterborne preservative treatments, ammoniacal copper zinc arsenate (ACZA) and ammoniacal copper quaternary ammonium (ACQ), do not contain chromium oxides. The performance of the stain on lumber treated with these chemicals will be similar to that of untreated wood, given similar finish coverage and exposure conditions. Occasionally, a small amount of powder residue may appear on the surface of treated wood. This powder is a residue of treatment chemicals and should be removed with a stiff bristle brush with soap and water before the finish is applied.

Several commercial wood treaters are using a water-repellant treatment combined with CCA treatment for 5/4 x 6 inch radius edge decking (RED). This lumber is marketed under trade names such as Ultrawood, Wolman Extra, and Weathershield. Although the water repellant is supposed to thoroughly saturate the wood, maintenance periodically during its service life is suggested. If lumber with this combined treatment is available at your lumber supplier, it is probably worth the extra cost. It is still advisable to treat the cut ends and holes, and to reapply WRP to the entire deck periodically.

Moisture Content

To achieve the best finish performance, wood should be finished at a moisture content close to its moisture content in service. This moisture content is typically about 12 percent for most areas of the continental United States. The moisture content of purchased lumber can be high for various reasons. Untreated lumber may be sold in the green state (i.e., still containing the water

Figure 59. Lap marks on wood finished with semitransparent stain.

that was in the living tree); treated wood, saturated during the treating process, may not have been dried before it was delivered to the job site; and/or the wood may have not been protected from wet weather before or after the deck was built. Although lumber should be at its in-service moisture content when it is finished, it is acceptable to finish the wood at moisture contents up to 20 percent, particularly if applying a penetrating finish. Penetrating finishes allow the wood to continue to dry.

Procedures for Finishing New Decks

The first finish that is applied to the wood, whether the structure is a deck or any other structure, is the most important. The moisture content of the wood should be below 20 percent before finishing. At this moisture content, the wood will feel dry to the touch. However, if the wood is extremely wet, such as undried pressure-treated wood, the surface may feel dry to the touch after 1 or 2 days in direct sunlight, but the internal moisture content may still be above 20 percent. The rate of drying depends on weather conditions; under warm and dry summer conditions, about 2 to 4 weeks should be sufficient. Keep in mind, however, that waiting too long will allow the wood surface to begin to weather enough to hinder the performance of a film-forming finish.

Penetrating Finishes

If you select a penetrating finish, the next decision is whether to use a semitransparent stain or a water-repellant preservative (WRP). The service life of a WRP is about 1 year on exposed surfaces. However, WRPs are extremely easy to reapply to decks. Because WRPs are not pigmented, problems with uneven wear and lap marks are eliminated (Fig. 59). The expected service

No coat   One coat   Two coats   Three coats   Four coats
                                                                 (top two coats did not absorb)

Figure 60. Effect of number of coats on finish appearance and absorption. Shiny areas (on right) caused by nonabsorbtion of semitransparent stain resulting from too many coats.

life of semitransparent stains is 2 to 3 years, but it can be much longer if the stain absorbs well.

If you are unsure about whether to use stain or WRP, you can always apply the WRP to the deck initially and then switch to a semitransparent stain when the deck needs to be refinished. Even if the deck has been maintained with a WRP for many years, a semitransparent stain will still perform satisfactorily because it penetrates the wood and does not fail by peeling as does a film-forming finish. It may be necessary to wait 2 or 3 months to finish lumber treated with a factory-applied water repellant. If the deck has been maintained with a WRP, it must age sufficiently for the stain to absorb properly.

Apply both WRPs and stains by brush or pad because this application method works the finish into the wood. To avoid lap marks (Fig. 59) in applying semitransparent stains, apply the stain the full length of only two or three boards at a time. Lap marks occur when the new finish overlaps the previously applied finish that has begun to dry. It is important to apply only as much stain as the wood will absorb. Do not puddle or pool excessive stain on the surface. The extra stain will appear as shiny areas on the surface (Fig. 60). For decay resistance and protection against mildew, an annual or even semiannual application of WRP formulated with a mildewcide should be effective.

Film-Forming Finishes

Although film-forming finishes are **not** recommended for decks, the following guidelines may improve service life. Finishing requirements are different for the decking portion (including stairs) and the railings.

Decking and stairs—The primary consideration in selecting a paint for the horizontal surfaces is abrasion resistance. Finishes formulated for these surfaces are usually classified as oil-based, urethane-modified alkyds or high-performance architectural coatings. For the best service life, apply a WRP before applying the primer paint (see previous section on Moisture Content). The WRP used must be labeled as having only about 1 percent water repellant so as not to interfere with the adhesion of primer paint. The labeling usually indicates that paint can be applied over the WRP after several days. The primer and two topcoats should be applied according to the directions, after the specified waiting period.

Railings—Abrasion resistance is not as important for the portions of the deck that are not subject to traffic. Therefore, there is a wider choice of paint finishes. As with the decking, a WRP should be applied first, followed by a primer paint and two paint topcoats. The primer and topcoats can be latex formulations; however an oil-based, stain-blocking primer should be used on redwood or western cedars. For these species, application of two coats of acrylic latex is suggested. The acrylic latex has better resistance to sunlight, but it lacks the abrasion resistance of the oil-based, urethane-modified alkyd paints.

5

▲ ▲

INSPECTION AND MAINTENANCE

A deck should be inspected annually. Most problems can be detected early enough for low-cost solutions. Critical areas of concern are those places where wood can remain wet or can trap water, such as the area between the deck and the house, joints, and areas continuously exposed to rain and/or snow.

On decks close to the ground where there is insufficient clearance for inspection, it is prudent to remove a few decking boards every few years and inspect the supporting structure.

Notched areas are more prone to decay than are unnotched areas and should be checked carefully. As a general rule, anywhere that the end-grain of lumber is in contact with another piece of lumber or rests directly on concrete, water wicks into the end-grain. The adjacent piece of lumber or the concrete then prevents the end-grain from drying (Fig. 61).

Inspection of Structural Components

This section describes methods for inspecting decking boards, posts, joists,

---

Problems to Look For
- Decay, rot, mold, stain, mildew
- Loose joints, splits
- Fastener and hardware corrosion
- Pitch, extractives bleed
- Iron stain

Inspection Methods
- Visual inspection
- Use of a probe, such as a screwdriver, knife, or pick

---

beams, and decking. Replacement of degraded parts may be necessary.

Deck Attachment

If the deck is not properly constructed, water will tend to get trapped between the deck and the house. Thus, the area between the deck and the house is quite susceptible to decay and should be checked thoroughly. Use a probe and look for signs of high moisture content evident by water-related blue or black stain, water on the sill plate in the house, fruiting bodies of fungi, carpenter

Figure 61. Stain from water wicking into end-grain of treated post near groundline.

ants, wet or damp wood, or any surface soft-
ening of untreated wood in the rim-joists or
siding of the house.

Posts

The section of a post at the groundline
is most susceptible to decay. Posts can be
easily checked for decayed wood by using
a probe, such as a knife, pick, or screwdriver
(Fig. 62). Use sufficient force to penetrate
the surface of the wood. Once through the
surface, the ease with which the probe penetrates into the post is an indication of the
condition of the wood. Compare the ease of
penetration of the probe at this location with
penetration at other aboveground parts of
the post. The same technique can be used
with other parts of the structure. Wood can
often be decayed internally but appear
sound at the surface.

Posts in contact with concrete footings
should be checked at the fastener. Other
areas of increased decay hazard are where
the post is attached to other parts of the
structure, such as beams, joists, and/or railings. Posts should also be checked for signs

of termites. If the wood is easily penetrated
with a probe, remove a small piece and
examine it more closely for termite tunnels.
If you find termite tunnels or tubes, consult
a professional exterminator.

Posts should be visually checked for
mold, mildew, carpenter ant invasion, fruiting bodies of fungi, and wet or damp wood.

Joists and Beams

Moisture can be trapped in many places
in joists and beams where two pieces of
wood are in contact. End-grain in contact
with other wood is a critical place to inspect,
using a probe. If the joists rest on top of the
beams, inspect the joists at all points of contact. Visually inspect for water stains, mold,
mildew, carpenter ants, fruiting bodies of
fungi, and wet or damp wood.

Decking

The easiest components of the deck to
inspect are the decking boards. Probe the
ends of the decking boards since they are
the areas most susceptible to decay. Butt-
joints of decking boards located over a
single joist and ends attached to a decking

Figure 62. Inspection of post at post-foundation fastener. Note erosion around footing resulting from improper landscaping.

board are particularly important to inspect (Fig. 58). Look for water stains and mildew growth, the warning signs of decay problems.

Inspection and Maintenance of Deck Finish

When inspecting the finish, look at finished areas that have high traffic or are fully exposed to sunlight. A change in color indicates erosion of the finish, fading as a result of sunlight, or the presence of mildew or other fungal growth.

A deck can keep its original appearance if maintained periodically. Maintenance may include light sanding to remove raised grain, washing to remove mildew, and re-application of a WRP or semitransparent stain.

The following text describes some problems that may be revealed during deck inspection and ways to correct the problems. These problems include raised grain, mold and mildew, iron stain, extractives bleed, and pitch.

Raised Grain

The wetting and drying cycles of wood exposed outdoors will usually result in rough surfaces caused by raised grain. On flat-grained lumber, raised grain may appear as thin, knife-like feathers along the earlywood-latewood interface. Sand these areas lightly to provide a suitable surface for the finish. Sand with the grain of the wood using 80- to 100-grit sandpaper. Refinish using a WRP or a semitransparent stain.

Mold and Mildew

Mold and mildew can grow on either untreated or preservative-treated wood. Annual treatment with a water repellant can keep the wood free of mold and mildew.

The most common discoloration caused by mold and mildew is a dull grey (Fig. 51). On untreated redwood or cedar, mildew sometimes has a black, blotchy appearance. In some climates such as along the seashore, wood tends to weather to a silver-grey. The weathering process removes the colored extractives and lignin, leaving only cellulose. The silver-grey discoloration is a combina-

Figure 63. Examples of iron stain (top) and extractives bleed (bottom) caused by fasteners in cedar.

tion of mildew and cellulose. Preservative-treated wood that has not been treated with a WRP will initially turn to a dull grey. Eventually, this wood will also change to silver-grey in some areas.

For the first few years of the deck's service life, the natural color of the wood can be partially restored by scrubbing the wood surface with a bleach/water mixture (see sidebar) or a commercial wood cleaner. Scrub the wood with a stiff bristle brush and rinse thoroughly with water. Allow the surface to dry for several days before refinishing. If the deck has been exposed for many years without a finish, much of the natural color in the surface of the wood has probably been leached out. The amount of color that returns after bleaching depends on how much the surface has weathered.

Iron Stain

Iron stain is caused by iron or steel in contact with wood. This type of discoloration results from fasteners and can also result from using steel wool or a wire brush on wood. Small particles of steel fibers or specks of rust embed in the wood, and the iron reacts with the tannins in the wood. This can cause an unsightly black stain; even a small amount of iron can result in a stain (Fig. 63). Avoid using iron-containing abrasives on outdoor wood.

Iron stains can be removed by washing the stained area with a saturated aqueous

---

How to Remove Mildew

Commercially available deck cleaners are quite effective for removing mildew and other stains on wood decks. A mildew cleaner can also be made from household liquid bleach and powdered laundry detergent in water. Suggested formula:

    1 qt (5 percent) sodium hypochlorite
      (household liquid bleach)
    1/3 c powdered laundry detergent
    3 qt warm water

CAUTION

DO NOT use a detergent that contains ammonia; ammonia reacts with bleach to form a poisonous gas. Many liquid detergents contain additives that react with bleach.

How to Remove Iron Stains

Saturate the stained area with a saturated solution of oxalic acid (1 lb./gal. hot water) and allow it to soak into the wood for several minutes. Rinse the area thoroughly and allow the wood to dry before refinishing. If the stain was caused by a fastener, remove the fastener before applying the oxalic acid to the wood. Replace this fastener with a noncorrosive fastener.

CAUTION

Oxalic acid is toxic. Avoid contact with the skin and do not ingest.

oxalic acid solution (see sidebar). If the wood has been finished with a stain or a water repellant, the water repellants in these finishes inhibit the discoloration, but the finish also tends to decrease the effectiveness of the oxalic acid treatment. Sometimes, the situation can only be corrected by replacing the problem boards and fasteners.

Extractive Bleeding

Another common cause of discoloration that is often mistaken for iron stain is the bleeding of extractives. This discoloration often occurs around fasteners because the hole in the wood caused by the fastener cuts across many wood cells (Fig. 63). These cut cells increase water absorption. Water dissolves the extractives and when the wood dries, the extractives accumulate at the surface. Sunlight causes them to polymerize. Although the bleeding of extractives can be a problem on wood railings, it is seldom a problem on the deck because the extractives are usually washed from the wood by rain before they polymerize.

Extractives can be removed by scrubbing the wood with soap and water. Do not use a wire brush because the brush will contaminate the surface with iron, resulting in iron stains. Finishing the deck with either a semitransparent stain or a WRP greatly minimizes extractive bleeding.

Pitch Bleeding

Pitch is the resinous substance that bleeds from the resin canals of some softwoods, such as pine and Douglas-fir. Pitch is normally set within the wood by high temperatures during the kiln-drying process. Often, when sunlight heats the surface of wood that has not been kiln-dried, pitch can bleed from some areas of the wood.

For small areas of pitch bleeding, you can scrape off the pitch, heat the wood with a heat lamp or hair dryer for a short time to encourage more pitch bleeding, and then dissolve and remove the heat-softened pitch with mineral spirits or turpentine. Repeating this process two or three times will often remove most of the resin so that the problem does not recur. For larger areas of pitch bleeding, the simplest solution is to replace the affected board. Boards with an area of pitch bleeding greater than a couple of square inches should be removed.

Recommendations for Refinishing

If mildew is present on the deck, pretreat the deck with a commercial deck cleaner or a household liquid bleach/water solution prior to refinishing the deck (see sidebar). Allow the deck to dry for 1 or 2 days after cleaning before refinishing. Be sure to follow the manufacturer's directions for temperature limitations because finishes do not cure properly if the temperature is too low.

If the deck has raised grain, light sanding may be necessary before applying the WRP. Sanding with 80- to 100-grit sandpaper, either manually or with a power sander, is usually adequate. Because the sanding dust may contain residual preservative, wear a dust mask while sanding and remove sanding dust from the wood before refinishing.

Apply a WRP using a brush, roller, or pad. The structural members do not need to be refinished as often as the exposed decking boards. Apply a liberal amount of WRP to decay-prone areas around fasteners and end-grain. If refinishing with a semitransparent stain, apply the stain evenly and wipe excess stain from areas where it does not penetrate.

Surfaces should be refinished when the wood starts to lose its color. The new finish needs to absorb into the wood. Finishing the wood too soon leads to inadequate absorption and film formation. Finishing the wood too late leads to excessive degradation of the wood surface.

Additional Sources of Information

This manual is intended to provide answers to many common questions on material for wood decks, treatments, design, and finishing. Because the manual does not address all issues, additional sources of information are as follows:

AF&PA
American Forest and Paper Association
1111–19th Street, NW, #800
Washington, DC 20036
202-463-2700

ALSC
American Lumber Standard Committee
P.O. Box 210
Germantown, MD 20875-0210
301-972-1700

ASTM
American Society for Testing and
  Materials
1916 Race Street
Philadelphia, PA 19103
215-299-5400

AWPA
American Wood Preservers' Association
P.O. Box 286
Woodstock, MD 21163-0286
410-465-3169

FPS
Forest Products Society
2801 Marshall Court
Madison, WI 53705
608-231-1361

CRA/RIS
California Redwood Association/Redwood
  Inspection Service
405 Enfrente Drive, Suite 200
Novato, CA 94949
415-382-0662

SFPA
Southern Forest Products Association
P.O. Box 641700
Kenner, LA 70064-1700
504-443-4464

USDA
U.S. Department of Agriculture,
  Forest Service
Forest Products Laboratory
One Gifford Pinchot Drive
Madison, WI 53705-2398
608-231-9200

WCLIB
West Coast Lumber Inspection Bureau
P.O. Box 23145
Tigard, OR 97281
503-639-0651

WRCLA
Western Red Cedar Lumber Association
1200-555 Burrard St.
Vancouver, British Columbia
Canada V7X 1S7
604-684-0266

WWPA
Western Wood Products Association
522 SW Fifth Avenue
Portland, OR 97204-2122
503-224-3930

GLOSSARY

Above-ground. Term used in the use-category classification system of the treated wood industry to describe treated lumber intended for low-to-moderate decay hazards, such as outdoor use when not in contact with the ground.

Ammoniacal copper quat (ACQ). Waterborne wood preservative containing copper and quat salt (didecyldimethylammonia chloride). Ammonia is added as a cosolvent to solubilize the copper and quat. ACQ is fully specified in AWPA Standard P-5, Sections 12 and 13.

Ammoniacal copper zinc arsenate (ACZA). Waterborne wood preservative containing copper, zinc, and arsenic. Ammonia is added as a cosolvent to solubilize the copper and zinc. ACZA is fully specified in AWPA Standard P-5, Section 3.

Annual growth ring. Layer of wood growth added to a tree during a single growing season.

Band joist. Also called rim or header joist. Two-by-x members used to frame in the ends of house floor joists. Decks are often attached to this structural member.

Beam. Structural member that transfers joist loads to posts of a deck.

Bracing. The 2x4 or 2x6 structural members used to reduce tendency of deck to rack or roll over.

Check. Lengthwise separation of wood that usually extends across annual growth rings and commonly results from stresses arising in wood during drying.

Chromated copper arsenate (CCA). Waterborne wood preservative containing chromium, copper, and arsenic. CCA is fully specified in AWPA Standard P-5, Sections 4, 5, and 6.

Cup. Type of warp. Flatwise deviation from straight line across width of a board.

Decay fungi. Wood-destroying fungi capable of biologically breaking down and metabolizing structure of wood. (Compare to mildew and mold, which are staining fungi that live in or on wood, but only metabolize nonstructural extractives.)

Decking board. Floor board of deck.

Dimension lumber. Lumber with nominal thickness of 2 to 5 inches and nominal width of 2 or more inches. Stress graded with design values for structural use.

Earlywood. Portion of annual growth ring formed during early part of growing season. Earlywood, also referred to as springwood, is usually less dense and mechanically weaker than latewood. (See Fig. 1.)

Edge-grained. Lumber that has been sawn parallel to the pith and approximately perpendicular to the growth rings. Grain as seen on cut made at right angle to direction of fibers (e.g., on cross-section of a tree). Also referred to as quarter-sawn or vertical-grained lumber. (See Fig. 2, a.)

Extractives. Substances in wood, not an integral part of the cellular structure, that can be removed by solution in hot or cold water, ether, benzene, or other solvents that do not react chemically with wood components.

Fastener. In this manual, generic term for nails, screws, bolts, and metal hardware used to connect deck members.

Flat-grained. Lumber that has been sawn parallel to pith and approximately tangent to growth rings. Lumber is considered flat grained when annual growth rings make an angle of less than 45° with the wide surface of the piece. Also referred to as plain-sawn or flat-sawn lumber. (See Fig. 2, c.)

Footing. Section used to support post to transfer deck loads to soil; usually made of concrete.

Framing. In this manual, generic term for beams, joists, posts, and other structural wood members of deck.

Freestanding. Deck that is self-supporting and not attached to house or other structure.

Fruiting body. On wood, this term refers to mushroom-like reproductive organs of decay fungi. Presence of fruiting bodies indicates advanced stage of wood decay.

Fungicide. Class of chemicals that are toxic to fungi. Chemicals to be sold and/or used in the United States as a fungicide must be approved by the U.S. Environmental Protection Agency (EPA).

Grade mark. Official identification on lumber that indicates grading agency, sawmill, grade, species, and moisture content at time of final manufacture.

Grading. (See Lumber grade.)

Ground contact. Term used in the use-category classification system of the treated wood industry to describe treated lumber intended for high-decay hazards, such as use in contact with the ground.

Growth ring. (See Annual growth ring.)

Heartwood. Wood extending from pith to sapwood. Heartwood cells no longer participate in life processes of the tree. Heartwood may contain extractives, phenolic compounds, gums, resins, and other materials that usually make it darker and more decay-resistant than sapwood.

Hot-dipped galvanizing. Single or double dipping of a fastener in molten zinc.

Incising. Perforation or knifelike slits created in surface of lumber species that are difficult to treat with preservatives. Incising creates hundreds of small openings per square foot of surface, which allow increased penetration of preservative.

Iron stain. Color change to wood resulting from reaction of iron or steel with tannins in the wood.

Joist. In this manual, wood structural member that supports decking boards and that spans between beams.

Juvenile wood. Wood, formed during first few years (8 to 10) of tree's growth, that surrounds pith center of tree. Referred to as pith-associated wood.

Kiln-dried after treatment (KDAT). Treated lumber that has been kiln-dried to below 19 percent moisture content after preservative treatment.

Knot. Portion of branch or limb that remains in lumber and is surrounded by adjacent growth of wood in the tree.

Lacquer. Clear, film-forming finish without an ultraviolet (UV) blocker to protect the underlying wood.

Lap mark. Finishing problem that occurs during application of a semitransparent stain; results from application of additional finish over the finish that has begun to dry.

Lateral load. Any horizontal load on the deck that tends to make the deck rack or roll over.

Latewood. Portion of annual growth ring formed after earlywood formation has ceased. Latewood, also referred to as summerwood, is usually denser and mechanically stronger than earlywood.

Longitudinal. Pertains to direction generally parallel to direction of wood fibers.

Lumber grade. Assessment of lumber quality, strength, and/or utility by a qualified, certified grader and assignment to a use-category. Lumber can be graded for strength or appearance.

Mildew. Black fungus that grows on surface of wood, causing the wood to darken with time.

Mildewcide. Chemical that is toxic specifically to mildew fungi.

Moisture content. Amount of water contained in the wood, usually expressed as a percentage of the weight of the ovendry wood.

Overhang. Portion of deck that extends beyond line of posts or beams; also called a cantilever.

Penetrating finish. Finish that penetrates a wood surface and does not form a film.

Pitch. Accumulation of resin from tree that may ooze from the wood when temperatures rise above previous wood temperatures.

Post. Structural member that supports the beam and transfers deck load to footing. Also called a column.

Post-treatment drying. (See Kiln-dried after treatment.)

Preservative. Chemical used to protect wood against decay.

Radial. Coincident with radius from axis of tree or log to circumference (i.e., line extending as a radius from pith center of tree to outer bark).

Radius edge decking (RED). Lumber produced specifically for decking, generally 1 inch thick and 5-1/2 inches wide, with eased (rounded) edges.

Railing. Portion of deck constructed for enclosure; includes rail post, cap rail, head rail, and balusters.

Relative humidity. Ratio of amount of water vapor present in air to that which the air would hold at saturation at the same temperature.

Retention. A measure of the amount of preservative injected into a standard, specified outer zone (i.e., assay zone) of wood. Retention of preservative is measured by chemical assay of that specified zone.

Sapwood. Light-colored wood near outside of log. Sapwood cells participate in the life processes of the tree. Under most conditions, sapwood is more susceptible to decay than heartwood.

Semitransparent stain. Penetrating water-repellant preservative finish that contains a pigment for color and protection from ultraviolet radiation.

Shelling. Separation or failure of wood along annual rings between earlywood and latewood bands.

SPF (spruce-pine-fir). Species combination for lumber grading and marketing.

Springwood. (See Earlywood.)

Stain. Bacterial: darkening of wood surface from mildew fungi. Wood finish: see Semitransparent stain.

Sticker. Thin wood slat used to separate layers of boards to facilitate drying.

Structural grade. (See Lumber grade.)

Summerwood. (See Latewood.)

Tangential. Line perpendicular to radial line and tangent to growth rings. Flat-grained lumber is sawn tangentially.

Treated lumber. Lumber pressure treated with an approved preservative under appropriate standards of the American Wood Preservers' Association (AWPA) or American Society for Testing and Materials (ASTM). Also referred to as preservative-treated lumber.

Treatment quality mark. Mark on treated lumber identifying and assuring that it has been produced under a quality-control program monitored by an independent, American Lumber Standards Committee (ALSC)-accredited, third-party inspection agency.

Treatment standards. Standards established by the American Wood Preservers' Association (AWPA) or American Society for Testing and Materials (ASTM) that detail acceptable preservative chemicals and appropriate retentions and penetrations for various treated wood products.

Tributary load. Portion of assumed uniform deck load carried by each structural member.

Uplift. Tendency for structural members to lift up as a result of lateral loads or structural instability.

Varnish. Clear, film-forming finish that does not contain an ultraviolet blocker for protecting wood.

Water-repellant finish. Finish that contains only a water-repellant chemical.

Water-repellant preservative (WRP). Finish that contains both a water-repellant chemical and a mildewcide.

Weathering. Photochemical degradation of wood surface combined with effects of ultraviolet radiation, water, and abrasion by wind-blown sand and other particulates.

INDEX

Pages with illustrations have their numbers in *italics*. Pages with tables have their numbers in **bold**.

Selection and Use of Preservative-Treated Wood

Wood is a biological material that is subject to decay, insect, and marine borer attack. These agents are nature's way of recycling wood and other biological materials in the natural ecosystem. Without nature's recycling system, we would literally be buried under piles of wood and other cellulosic materials such as grass, leaves, and agricultural residues. However, when wood is used in applications that are designed to last, it must be protected from biological deterioration. This book was written for homeowners, contractors, building supply personnel, architects, and any other individuals who use or recommend the use of wood products in applications where deterioration may be a factor.

This book provides an in-depth discussion of the causes and types of wood deterioration, the degree of protection needed in various applications, and the types of preservative systems available. Also covered in this book are material and treatment specifications, post-construction inspections, remedial treatments, finishing of treated wood and safety and environmental issues. Detailed information is supplied for specific applications of treated wood from playground structures to permanent wood foundations, and a comprehensive list of sources of information on treated wood is provided.

Chapters included are:

To order Selection and Use of Preservative-Treated Wood for the list price of $24.95 (price includes shipping and handling) contact the Forest Products Society, 2801 Marshall Court, Madison, WI 53705-2295 or telephone (608) 231-1361. Credit card orders and orders to be invoiced may use FAX number (608) 231-2152.